Good Days & Great Days

Walking the South West Coastal Path
and other Worldwide Adventures

Ross Bullock

Published by Bullocks Publications, Leigh, Greater Manchester

Every effort has been made to obtain the necessary permissions with reference to copyright material both illustrative and quoted. We apologise for any omissions in this respect and will be pleased to make the appropriate acknowledgements in any future edition.

Printed by The Print Room, Bolton
info@the-print-room.co.uk

A catalogue record for this book is available from the British Library

ISBN 978-1-5262-0574-2

www.rossbullock.com

For Elaine, who has always tried to keep me on the straight and narrow.

Contents

Contents

Foreword

THE OLD HOLLYWOOD FILM casting system used to catalogue the "extras" by type.

You know, "Young Englishman No.24" or "Elderly shopkeeper No.83". If that categorisation still applied, Ross Bullock would probably be "Traditional Bank Manager No.12".

However, typecasting anyone – and particularly Ross – would be a great mistake. He still looks the bank manager that he was for many years, a serious and knowledgeable professional keen to represent and protect the establishment while genuinely trying to help the customer. But he is actually quite a different character these days, and this book reflects it.

He loves walking. He has always loved walking, in the countryside, in towns and villages and along the many coastal paths this country boasts in abundance.

That in itself might be enough to fascinate many people, perhaps similar lovers of English rural life who appreciate the green and pleasant vistas around the corner of every field or path. What makes Ross rather different is a quirky eye, a wicked sense of humour and a love of the essence of any place – be it South-west England or the glorious land and seascapes of New Zealand and the Cook Islands.

He writes as he talks: offering insights into the history of areas, milestones and trends of the time, what was in the news and what was happening to us more ordinary folk.

All this is, of course, enhanced by the fact that this particular "walk" was no summer jaunt over a few weeks or even a few months. This was a journey over many years, allowing time to pass and further memories and reminiscences to be involved. So the journey he took, that meanders through this enjoyable and gentle book, is really like wandering through time as well as accompanying him on a walk through some of this country's most stunning scenery.

Like the journey itself, it's possible to pick it up, read and absorb one stage of the low-key adventure involved. Then you can return to it on another occasion and feel that you are simply resuming a lovely dream – albeit outdoors, in beautiful countryside and in the company of a familiar friend who shares your interest in places and people.

The observations are sometimes random, sometimes linked to surroundings or a future destination, but they are always entertaining and absorbing. It's like a friendly voice in your ear, discussing all the subjects that interest you and adding anecdotes to suit the moment.

Please don't expect a highly detailed travel itinerary – or indeed anything similar to any walking book you have ever read. Ross Bullock, in spite of the genuine possibility of typecasting, is a one-off, a classic English eccentric in the nicest possible way.

And if you're looking for a reflection on the best and most entertaining of walking trips you might ever take, this little book might just become your personal outdoors' companion.

Angela Kelly
Freelance Journalist & Media Consultant

Acknowledgements

FIRSTLY WE SHOULD ALL be grateful to Philip Carter and his wife Mary. History sees them as being largely responsible in turning what was a generally unsigned, blocked and often overgrown former Coastguard's path in the south west of England into what is now a national treasure, giving enjoyment to millions of people every year.

On a more personal level I must thank Bernard Hedley for painstakingly proof reading the book, transforming it into a format for printing, as well as making invaluable editorial suggestions. To Sue Wallace, who produced the excellent cartoons contained herein. She is an active supporter of Action for Children, who do superb work in helping young and vulnerable children build their self-esteem and confidence. Also to Rob Waddington for the imaginative, and I hope you find, amusing front cover to the book.

And where would I be without Garry and Peter from the Print Room in Bolton, for their superb work in production of this book. When they got together, almost at the same time as I was taking my first steps on the Path, I told them that partnerships rarely work out. Clearly this one has, and in true honesty, they still have not a clue why it has been such a success. I can tell them, in quite simple terms, that they offer and provide, an outstanding service to their customers.

I am grateful also to my wife Elaine, who often trades as MB Taxis, for transporting me around the country, whether it be to the airport, or to the start or at the end of each day's trail when needed. And she never charged me once! It was her father, Les, whose story is contained within these pages, made me want to write more. What he achieved in the Second World War fighting for his country, put my achievement on this walk into pale insignificance.

Acknowledgements

Finally I wish to thank, in a big way, Colin. He was always incredibly supportive of me in my banking days, and especially when things were not going well. For this walk, not only did he let me get on with the planning process, but he put up with me along the way without complaint. I never enjoy walking on my own, and his companionship throughout proved invaluable and contributed to my enjoyment of the Path more than words can ever express.

PART ONE

SOUTH WEST
COASTAL PATH

CHAPTER 1

A Good Beginning

IT HAS BEEN SAID, and I totally agree, that your whole life hangs on a thread.

In my case, it was Christmas 2002, when my old (and last) boss in ye olde Midland Bank, Colin Billington, put on his Christmas Card to me "Do you fancy doing a bit of the South West Coastal Path with me next year?" I had left the Bank in 1997 and he did in 1998 and had emigrated to Dorset, but we had kept in touch. He knew I was a keen walker, and in fact had joined me on one or two of my long distance trails in previous years. In fact he was nearly banned once for turning up in Leeds wearing pink socks.

Now I would like to think of myself as being an "all or nothing" sort of chap. I certainly don't do 'bits' and love a challenge, and this certainly became one. The South West Coastal Path (SWCP) is England's longest waymarked footpath stretching from Minehead in Somerset, to Poole in Dorset. Officially a mere 630 miles, cliff slippage and erosion along the way, never mind negotiation of estuaries in South Devon, makes this figure debatable, but nevertheless impressive. The total height climbed also varies, but let's say a mere 115,000ft, which in itself is like climbing Everest (from sea level) four times.

On average folk take 52 days to complete the walk, usually in stages. The record, at the time of writing, belongs to a 53 year old chap called Mark Berry, who **ran** it. It took him a 11 days, 8 hours and 15 minutes. He was reported at the time, because he beat an existing record of some 14 days or something, to have been 'absolutely elated'. I bet he was.

Some people (no names mentioned) take a bit longer, passing by some 2,473 signposts or waymarks, going through 921 stiles (431 of which are of the kissing gate variety) and passing over some 302 bridges, to make it to the end. It costs about £1000 per mile to keep the paths open, maintain them, and ensure they are clearly signposted.

As we were both still working fulltime, we agreed to do a stretch each year, invariably of four days usually happening in early May. In total it took us 58 days, stretching over 14 years. I reckon it will have involved me in over 9,000 miles of driving, and we will have probably stayed in over 50 establishments, varying from one or two grotty bed and breakfasts, some excellent ones, guest houses/pubs and where geography dictated, some Hotels. Indeed, research has indicated that in 2014, walkers on the path spent about £468m, and it sustained some 10,610 full-time jobs. You have to agree these are pretty staggering figures. And at the end of some of the days we walked, boy, was I also staggering.

The SWCP Association, formed in 1973, does a fine job in supporting the interests of users of the path, as well as producing an excellent annual guide to help in the planning process. Colin was more than happy for me to perform this process, and as my former boss, he would quite rightly have probably delegated it to me anyway.

Those of you out there, who know me, will know I love a challenge, and have written about my previous long distance walks, which were invariably for charity raising purposes. Always involving helping children, this time I have chosen

Donna's Dream House Charity in Blackpool. They provide free holiday experiences for children with life-threatening illnesses and their families, and for recently bereaved siblings and their families. Operated by volunteers only, 99p of each pound I can raise will be used to provide the holiday costs plus related support work.

For this walk, and unusually for me, I have only a few notes to refer to, and as such I have to rely on an occasionally failing memory, and the hundreds of pictures I took. And a lot happened in those 14 years, as you would expect, much of which I wish to record now. Subscribers to the Association's regular magazine often write in to share experiences, good and rarely bad, and without exception say how much they enjoyed it. In my case the SWCP has been an incredible part of my life, please read on. I hope you won't be disappointed.

CHAPTER 2

2003
Minehead to Ilfracombe

O N 21ST AUGUST, 2003 it all started off. This suited Colin, as he had used some of his savings to treat his wife and eight year old daughter, to a week in Butlin's nearby. He was still full of it as we queued for butties before locating the official start point for the walk. And, if you believe what I have just written, you might as well believe they landed on the Moon in 1969. We had our picture taken in front of an impressive metal sculpture, with two severed hands opening a map of the peninsula. A local church clock chimed at one o'clock, and we were off!

A search of the internet reveals no mention of this auspicious landmark, but in this year we invaded Iraq, Apple launched iTunes and Dennis Thatcher, bless him, died.

After a steep climb we were onto Exmoor National Park, where we saw lots of ponies and antlers, but very little of the sea. In what seemed no time at all, we were going down into Porlock and our first night together, before which we visited a fine pub, the Ship Inn. Bizarrely (how I love the word) I think this was the first time I had had a drink with Colin, and not having seen him for years, had lots to share. He is a fine listener, and it was a great time spent there. 'Men talk' at its best, and still a lot about banking, as you would expect. Our conversation also drifted to talking about the death of Dr David Kelly, who had died a month earlier. Now if he committed suicide I am an ardent Manchester United fan who loves shopping, cycling, all the Soaps and Brussel sprouts.

Our first B&B was a thatched cottage on the main street, and bizarrely (OK I will not use it again) our room was in the roof, which you got to literally by climbing up some steep steps. I don't think I had ever seen a former Midland Bank Area Manager on his hands and knees before, nor since come to think of it. A great evening meal followed at a local restaurant, with the scene set for the period, for me invariably on the red meat and Colin the fish. This was the first time we had slept together and there were no incidents of note.

Our pleasant landlady we had seen in the pub the night before, and she cooked a pleasant breakfast the next morning. No sign of Mr B&B, more of which later.

Day 2. Only 625 miles to go, and the walk started in earnest. The Association superbly advises on each days walk, the length, the ascent and grading, which are named: easy, moderate, strenuous or severe. All very subjective, of course. How can a 20 mile 'easy walk', for instance, be easy? Come to think of it, all these years later, I don't remember many easy days on the Path at all.

This day was to be a 15 miles 'moderate' walk being strenuous in parts, ending up in Lynmouth Harbour, with ascent of some 3,000 feet. After an 'easy' start, when I actually saw the sea and Wales (the country not a spelling error) across the Bristol Channel, there was a major incident.

I love the outdoors, and adventure. Striding Edge and Swirral Edge on Helvellyn were great, and I thoroughly enjoyed them both. Probably the hairiest I have experienced was Sharp Edge on Blencathra. On the latter, when we were ambling through Thelkeld on the way up, some cheerful Cumbrian farmer advised us that "some old bloke died on Sharp Edge last week, y'know".

And many years later, there I was strolling along the South West Coastal Path, in some woods above Porlock Weir, when

I fell off! In a millisecond my chin was on the path, and my feet dangling somewhere over the abyss below, clinging on for dear life, when Colin exclaimed the immortal words "Don't move!!" Not that I blumin' could.

You will appreciate, that as former bankers we had done a Risk Assessment of the walk, and I was the appointed First Aider, and therefore carried the plasters and hip flask. Colin, now thrust into this role without any training, quickly worked out that as we were about a mile inland there was no danger of me falling into the sea, and therefore spoiling his walk, and as I was breathing quite easily there was no need for him to administer mouth to mouth resuscitation. And with my feet quickly locating a small ledge below, I was able to clamber up quite easily with Colin's help and all was well again.

We soon came upon Culbone Church, the smallest complete parish church in England, being some 35 feet by 12 feet 4 inches to be exact, and built in the 12th century and still in superb nick, and would be full to bursting with 30 persons in the congregation. A framed placard reads: "For nearly 1000 years, as shepherds put their mark on their lambs, so children of the Good Shepherd have been baptised at this font". I was quite touched when Colin climbed the pulpit, and uttered a short prayer of thanksgiving that we were still together and able to continue the walk. Little did he know what was to follow the next day. He also vowed to return with his own placard, and which would read: "Today was almost a step too far for my one-eyed friend, but thankfully he saw his way up and back to lead me on to pastures new" CTB 22 August 2003.

I loved reading Bill Bryson's 'Notes from a Small Island' and immediately purchased his next book namely "A Walk in the Woods" about his abortive attempt to walk the world's longest footpath, namely the 2,200 mile long Appalachian Trail, which, in contrast, thoroughly disappointed. It may be that I see little enjoyment in plodding mile after mile through woodland, with one tree looking pretty much like the next, only occasional glimpses of a blue sky above, precious little sun and on this stretch few views of the sea to our right. I was still not getting the feeling I was on a coastal walk.

Funnily enough, I read about Bryson being menaced by bears on the Trail. He was mugged at knifepoint in Johannesburg and narrowly survived killer spiders in Australia. Once asked what he would cite as the terrifying thought that really keeps him awake at night he replied "Being stuck in a broken lift with Piers Morgan and Janet Street-Porter". Superb, and I can but wholeheartedly agree with him.

Thankfully as we plodded westwards we saw Foreland

Point, and the ups and downs started (strenuous) and our destination of Lynmouth came into view, and later the hotel where we were to stay the night. And yes, there is nothing better after a long days walk to lounge in a deep bath, looking for the plastic duck, and contemplating the day's achievements. Except the **Bath** Hotel, where we were staying, only had a very average shower in the room.

Lynmouth is unfortunately more remembered for a disaster in August 1952 when torrential rains caused local rivers to overflow and sweep violently down causing devastation along the way, and regrettably 34 people died, and 420 made homeless. There is a conspiracy theory here that secret cloud seeding experiments carried out by the RAF nearby caused the heavy rain. I can't possibly comment.

Day 3. Another fine day beckoned, and a tough walk to Combe Martin, 13 miles away. It was a steep climb up alongside the town's cliff railway, which is over 110 years old. Reportedly you take a ride on it if you want a bit of fun. It is driven by the weight of water in the tank of the down-coming car. When the car reaches the bottom, the water is emptied out and the car at the top has its tank filled until it starts its slow downward descent, pulling the other car to the top.

And what a fun day it was for us too, in that it had everything, including a lunchtime pub. In the woods above Lynton, we came across a pleasant local couple walking their dog, who asked us what we were up to. The lady then espied a caricature picture of me on Colin's T-Shirt, one we got produced when we were walking the Leeds and Liverpool canal, and exclaimed, looking at me quizzically, "Are you a Vicar then?". Much laughter ensued. Now with my name I have been called many things in my life, but Vicar! Thereafter, in deference to my new career, Colin still calls me Vic, and I call him Bish, often more correctly the Bishop of Sherborne.

We soon passed through the iconic Valley of Rocks, almost

without noticing them and falling in the 'much ado about nothing' category. In fact of more interest are the feral goats who nibble anything they can in the area, and in winter go down into Lynton and do similar deeds in the parks and gardens of the town, much to the annoyance of the locals. Needless to say that day, we didn't see any goats.

We soon passed a signpost in a cottage garden, which indicated Iceland one way, and New Zealand the other. All I wanted was to see a sign that read 'Combe Martin ¼ mile'. As it was it was over 11 miles, and as the day progressed, I had the feeling we had really arrived on the SWCP and this was what it was all about. The views down the coast and the Bristol Channel were stunning, the freshness of the wind as we walked along some of the highest cliffs of the Path exhilarating, and I will never forget the vibrant colour of pink and yellow heather on Holdstone Down.

But walking is what it was all about, and for most of the day it was like life, in that it has its ups and downs. What didn't seem far by eye invariably meant a severe trek down, and yes, you got it, an equally daunting climb up on the other side. I got to dread any downward steps because you knew what that meant. By the time we got to the Hunter's Inn, up from Heddon's Mouth I felt weary, and daren't look at the map as we were not even half way through the day, and the weather was getting even better.

I recall drinking some water from a pleasant stream, with Bish reminding me that it could contain sheep piss, and picking up on my little radio that my beloved Manchester City had only drawn 1-1 with Portsmouth at our first ever league encounter at the magnificent then named City of Manchester Stadium, with our right full back equalising five minutes from the end. Typical City!

Little did I know at the time, but we were at the foot of the Great Hangman, at 1043 ft, the highest point of the whole walk. The name has nothing to do with capital punishment or sheep stealing, but is of Celtic origin. As we trudged up and up I had to remind myself I was doing this walk for pleasure, and no one had forced me to do it. At the top we saw, for the first time, Lundy Island, and looked down on Combe Martin totally engulfed in sea mist, and passing by Little Hangman, Hangman Point, and the Hangman Pub, we staggered in to the town tired beyond belief, but in a strange way, how do I say it....'fulfilled?'

Day 4. Our B&B was ok, but I was appreciative of the owner, who had looked after my car, which I had dropped off there on Thursday. My eternal memory is, however, of Mr B&B collecting our breakfasts from a hatch, which was in between the kitchen and dining room. Hands up those of you out there remember hatches? Nowadays you just knock the whole wall down, or never have one in the first place.

A pleasant enough place, Combe Martin's origins were in lead and silver mining, and claims to have the second longest village street in the country. Can you possibly guess where is the first?

Today was to be a relatively easier day to Woolacombe, but with us both feeling the aftershock of the previous day's exertion we only got as far as Ilfracombe, a mere 7 miles away with little to report en route except tiredness. It was probably then some 45 years since I last had been there. I think we were living in Wolverhampton at the time, and travelled down through the night for a holiday in my Dad's old Ford. Naturally it was black. My brother and I had to sit on the suitcase on the back seat as it couldn't fit in the boot. I think this added to the adventure of the journey, but I have had a flat head ever since. No ordinary suitcase, of course, real leather (as they didn't do false 'real leather' then) it had been my Dad's during the Second World War, with a sign on it that it was Her Majesty's Government property.

The town itself seems to get bad press now, being either downbeat or downright rough. Whilst I enjoyed our ice cream on a bench in the harbour, there were just far too many people there for my liking, tourists I think they call them, and I had had enough anyway. Adventure over for the year, back to work and good old Bolton Council. Total distance covered was an underwhelming 40 miles.

And, should you still be wondering, it's Stewkley, in Buckinghamshire.

CHAPTER 3

2004
Ilfracombe to Instow

TWENTY YEARS EARLIER, as a mere lad, being of sound mind and body, I was awarded the degree 'Master of Ye Ancient Order of Barking Dogs' and still have the certificate to prove it. On 12 May 1984 I walked from Keswick to Barrow for charity, a distance of 40 miles all within the county of Cumbria, in just over 12 hours, and in trainers too!

This was an annual pilgrimage, which raised money for hospitals in Blackpool, and if you finished you received two free pints at the Vickers Social Club in Barrow. I had tried to do it the year before, but gave up after only 27 miles. I was as sick as the proverbial parrot. I was gutted, felt sick and deflated, but most of all I felt a failure.

In 1984 I enlisted the companionship of an old school chum, who happened to be a mean marathon runner. He was to be my inspiration, my mentor, my Svengali. I will, however, never forget the last three miles into Barrow. The kind folk of the town with houses adjoining the route had come out to offer us encouragement, drinks and whatever, and with plaintiff cries of "Come on, not far to go now". But you knew bloody well there were still three miles to go. Fellow walkers were literally clinging onto garden walls for support, with others in tears because they simply could no longer put one foot in front of another. Eventually we staggered into the Social Club, with the Notice Board indicating that someone (some freak?) had done the walk (ran it?) in 4 hours and 20 minutes.

I was then greeted by a truly wonderful beefy nurse, who took me in her ample arms, sat me down, and then bathed and massaged my aching feet in a bowl of warm water. A simple experience I have clearly never forgotten, I then looked up and was handed a pint of beer, with a superb head and taste to match. If I was in heaven I would have taken it there and then. As Benjamin Franklin once said "Beer is the proof God loves us and wants us to be happy"

This year saw the Olympics in Athens, which I guess they are still paying for, and his Holiness Tony Blair visited Gaddaffi in return for the dismantling of Libya's weapons of mass destruction. And we all know what an expert he became on the subject of WoMD. Google released Gmail. Thankfully, that bar steward Harold Shipman killed himself, and Brian Clough and John Peel died.

Day 5. The Bishop of Sherborne appeared suitably attired as we made our second attempt to reach Woolacombe, complete with new cassock with purple buttons, as we left Ilfracombe with few regrets. A fine day it was too, and with 2,037 feet of climbing in seven miles, certainly no walk over (sorry). All good, though, and we soon reached the lighthouse at Bull Point, walking on grass topped cliffs.

I can't recall ever climbing a lighthouse, even though I just love heights. The nearest similar climb would have been the 296 steps to the top of the Leaning Tower of Pisa. Now there's a classic example of how to turn a negative into a positive. I didn't see much from the top other than loads of steel erections to stop people jumping off. I saw no signs of any nearby Pisa Hut either.

Round the dark jagged rocks of Morte Point we espied Woolacombe (meaning 'Valley of the Wolves') and its fine sandy beach. It seemed like for the first time in nearly 50 miles we were on a beach, and it was full of strangely clad people dressed in multi-coloured leotards with black skin tight hats, clutching coffin shaped brightly painted pieces of plywood, running in and out of the sea like their lives depended on it. Bish told me that this was a local custom called surfing, and that I shouldn't confuse it with the surfing I did on the net, looking for such things as accommodation on the SWCP. It did, however, look quite exhilarating, and something I have never done. Somehow I don't think it will catch on in Southport.

Coincidentally as I write this Woolacombe beach has been named by travellers as the UK's best beach for the second year in a row, and one reviewer said he had been going there since 1950, and raved about the clean sand, beach huts for hire, three miles to walk the length and fantastic clifftop walks, making it for him a very special place. As a fellow pensioner, how can I possibly argue?

Over my years of walking I have stayed in many Bed & Breakfasts, and a bit like walkers themselves they come in many shapes and sizes, and usually of the husband and wife variety. Mr B&B usually does the meet and greet, admin, and waiting on, whilst Mrs B&B the cooking and I guess, the cleaning. Booking them for our walk was made easier through listing in the Association's annual publication, which indicates facilities and distance from the path. Usually easy to find, and invariably called Sea View Bed and Breakfast or something like that, I can be vexed if I see a sign outside which reads 'Walkers Please Take Your Boots Off before Entering these Premises'. As if I wouldn't. And having judged the owner and the place before words are exchanged, the first thing you look at when entering your allocated room is its size, how close the beds are to each other, whether there is a shower or bath, and was there a television and tea making facilities.

Having trudged half a mile up the imaginatively named Shore Road, I immediately didn't warm to Mr B&B, who failed miserably the 15 second rule. By way of research I asked him where was best to eat that evening; he replied by advising they were all great. This generally means they are all crap, and where we dined at the top of the hill, was, yes you've got it….it was crap and full of small persons running around and misbehaving. In our room, with the tea making facilities was a note saying that if more sachets of tea or coffee (there were 4 in total) were required, additional ones could be purchased from the owners, for 10p each! And to cap it all, when I was paying the next morning, engaging in the usual small talk like you do, Mr B&B advised that generally he didn't like accommodating walkers as they generally only stayed one night and moved on! Well, would you believe that?

I shared later with Bish my thoughts about our host and we both agreed….what a misery guts.

Day 6. Another fine day beckoned, and a relatively easy 15 mile stroll to Braunton was in prospect. Certainly it was great walking on and alongside Woolacombe Beach, and over to Baggy Point was equally satisfying. At the point was a totem pole, about 15ft tall which I took great delight in climbing to the top. The Bishop kindly took a picture, and which became well known in Bolton Council circles as 'Rusty's Column' (long story) but surprisingly never recognised by the National Trust on whose land it stood.

Soon we were down on the beach at Croyde Bay, and across the sand in no time. Being a Saturday it was full of those surfing persons, and plans were afoot for some form of open air pop concert, making the place noisy and busy. No time to linger we reached Saunton Sands, with superb sea views and lots of sand too. There was a great café there where we enjoyed a smashing hour, full of more men-talk and the meaning of life stuff. Bish was concerned about declining congregations, whilst I was more concerned about the number of accounts the Bank had lost since we left, and how it was affecting the Share Price.

The rest of the day was vaguely interesting, but hard work as we passed through a nature reserve, patchy woodland, the edge of a golf course and a military training area. We then walked along a dirt track for two miles, and then clung to the side of the river estuary until reaching the George Hotel in Braunton, also our overnight stop. Nothing to report other than it was really a pub, and a noisy average one at that.

Day 7. If there has to be a bad day on the Path, it has to be this stretch to Instow. In fact many walkers just miss it out and get the bus to Westward **Ho!** And for those suffering from Vertigo, the total ascent for the day is 52 feet. If I say the highlight of the day, other than the end, was the Lamb Burger and chips I had at the Wetherspoons in Barnstaple, you will get the message.

Why? Quite simply the route follows an old railway track that has been tarmacked in. And to make it worse, being a Sunday, not only was the route festooned with 'amateur' walkers with small children and dogs, there were hundreds of cyclists as this formed part of a recognised cycle route, which, of course, has national approval.

Thankfully the last mile was along the sands at Instow, but I finished with blisters, no stick which I had left somewhere en route, and with that feeling, 'Thank goodness that's done'.

To cap it all, I spent the evening on my own in the Commodore Hotel, as Bish had driven home for Evensong. A smashing colonial type building, there was some event on, and I ate alone in my room. Never the best with my own company, it was a very long evening. Even the beer was crap.

76 miles done, only 554 left.

CHAPTER 4

2005
Appledore to Hartland Quay

I N THIS YEAR Charles married CPB, and the Glaziers
gained control of Manchester United (why am I telling you
this?) and then mortgaged the place to pay back the loan they
had taken out to buy it, putting the Club heavily in debt, and
then allegedly took hefty management fees to cover the time
working out this fiddle to make it legal. Pubs were given
licence to open for 24 hours a day (good and bad in that
methinks). George Best died.

This year was a relatively short and straightforward stretch
from Appledore, which is across the River Taw Estuary, to
Hartland Quay.

Day 8. Bish and I met up in Westward **Ho!** and, quite
unusually for a distance walk we did a circular walk to
Appledore and back. Famous for its shipyard, which has gone
bust a few times but keeps bobbling back up, I just love the
place. From its position by the estuary, it has a maze of narrow
lanes, brightly coloured cottages, often decorated with
hanging baskets, one of which I could have purchased (the
cottage that is) if I had the odd two hundred thousand pounds
on me. The Beaver Inn wasn't bad either.

Day 9. Westward **Ho!** is the only place in the country to have an exclamation mark in its name. Charles Kingsley, from whose novel the town took its name, visited the place once and didn't like it. I hear that the residents didn't like the book much either. The title, I believe, derives from calls from the shores of the Thames in London to boat taxis with "eastward ho!" and "westward ho!" My memory of the town is of a line of beach huts, loads of litter bins and tacky gift shops. I had more exciting places to visit, and one of them was a tough 11 miles down the coast, namely Clovelly.

There is not a lot on this section other than undulating cliffs and substantial valleys as we moved into more boring woods. Surprisingly the last three miles is along an old carriage road known as Hobby Drive. Over 200 years old, it was built by locals to give them work after the Napoleonic Wars, and along which we got great glimpses of Bideford Bay, and the harbour at Clovelly. Bish took a picture of me grooving away on my new iPod, and using my walking stick as a pretend microphone. I believe the song was one of my favourites, Telegraph Road by Dire Straits. I looked particularly happy, which I indeed was.

To say Clovelly is unique is an understatement. It is simply awesome, and often referred to as one of the most beautiful villages in the country. We didn't have to pay to get in, but it is now £6 per person (no concessions!) and that has ruffled a few feathers I believe, but many of the residents are happy because it keeps tourists away. And if you fancy buying one of the 80 properties there, well you can't, because they are all owned by a chap called John Rous, a descendent of the Hamlyn family. We enjoyed our stay at the New Inn, on the village's iconic main cobbled street with white cottages, all seemingly having lichen covered slate roofs. Whilst having breakfast it was amusing to see goods being delivered, being pulled down on a sledge from the upper car park, whilst refuse is pulled further down the hill to the harbour for collection.

Day 10. There is basically not a lot between Clovelly and Hartland Quay, other than 11 miles and 2,382ft of ascent, and the defining headland of Hartland Point which had a great café, and where we turned left and southward for the first time. And for me to praise a café, it has to be something special.

I was, by now, well getting the hang of this coastal walking, especially on the north coast. Ambling along high headlands, occasionally daunting, with a gentle wind in your face and superb views all around, is simply brilliant. Occasionally I would say to Bish, in no uncertain terms, "STOP!". Whilst it is great telling your old boss what to do, more significantly was that it was usually a great view point, and where the only sound was the sound of nature, with waves smashing on to rocks, gentle winds or occasional bird sounds. For a second or two, it often seemed that nothing else in the world mattered.

Then there is the other side, and in this part of the world it is called a 'combe'. The way ahead would seem quite straightforward, then suddenly there was a path down, sometimes to the sea itself. Often the path would wind down to a thin line of vegetation that followed a stream to a beach, invariably via a small waterfall. Usually there were stepping stones, sometimes a weathered wooden bridge. In many instances you stopped, took on water, and started the ascent on the other side.

Eventually you would get to the top, and yes you've got the hang of this, you would soon be going down again and the whole process would repeat itself. Thankfully you sort of get used to it, and no one had forced us to do this walk anyway.

Hartland Quay is remote to say the least, and with views that seemed to stretch all the way down the Cornish coast. There was a superb sunset, which Bish took some great pictures of with his new self-focusing Brownie camera. The local brass band played in the courtyard in front of the hotel where we stayed, adding to the atmosphere, and I felt a little sad that our adventure was over for another year. All spoilt, for a moment anyway, whilst enjoying a pint in the bar, when I espied a picture of the Manchester United team lifting the European Cup, or whatever it was called. As they often say, every silver lining has a cloud.

CHAPTER 5

2006
Hartland Quay to Crackington Haven

PART OF THE PLEASURE I find in long distance walking is the planning process. Whilst my present wife calls me a 'control freak', to which I naturally object, I do like organising rather than being organised. My day walks, naturally, always and without exception, involve a pub stop at the halfway point. I have no problem, either, with 'linear walks', whereby you walk one way to a half way point, and turn back and return the same way. The ups become downs, or vice versa, the views are completely different, and, as expected, it is hard to get lost. More so, if the pub at the turning point serves Black Sheep, who possibly can object?

Planning for this year changed when the Association guide book arrived, in that they had many complaints (I use the word in humour) that the 16 mile (severe) stretch, with over 4,000 feet in ascent, from Hartland Quay to Bude, was proving to be a bit too much, and the local branch of International Rescue were being overworked in lifting stranded and exhausted walkers to safety. Indeed, there is always the argument that walks like this, over great distances, can become a bit of a route march, and that you don't always get time to actually enjoy what you're supposed to be enjoying. So Plan B kicked in.

This year saw the end of Grandstand after a 50 year stand, and we lost on penalties in the World Cup in Germany to Portugal. We had a heatwave, which was even hotter than we experienced in 1983, and Freddie Laker died.

I am a Freddie fan, just like Margaret Thatcher was, I believe. His life is well documented. In the early 1980's he championed the first low cost, no frills airline, primarily with Cross Atlantic flights. Later it was proven that the major airlines of the time had ganged up on him undercutting his fares, but 1981-2 was also the time of rising oil prices and recession. Most of all, however, was the effect of the falling pound in that all his loans (he had 27 banks lending to him by then) were in dollars and all his income was mainly in sterling. This was the final straw, and in 1982 Receivers were appointed.

That year I was transferred to that London and Midland Bank was one of his creditors. It was my responsibility at the time to write to him and explain the Bank's position in such circumstances. Two weeks later, in a handwritten letter on Basildon Bond paper, addressed to Mr Bullock, was his response. Its content would have delighted even the most hardnosed banker. To the Bank, here was a man of his word, and totally unlike many so called 'Entrepreneurs' who I encountered in my later banking career. He is up there with many of my heroes in the business world, and which includes the likes of Bill Gates, Steve Jobs, James Caan and James Dyson. To this day, I don't know why I didn't keep a copy of his letter.

Day 11. From Hartland Quay I decided we would stay halfway to Bude at Morwenstow. It is arguably the toughest section of the whole walk, and we were not for arguing as we crossed one river valley after another. Great jagged ridges of rock stretched out into the Atlantic, and a highlight of crossing into Cornwall at Marsland Mouth went almost unnoticed, although the pasties would soon be a calling. Thankfully it was another fine sunny day as we diverted up into the village of Morwenstow for our overnight stop.

A great place, with lovely old church, with such a hazardous coast nearby, the corpses of many drowned sailors were laid out in the churchyard before being buried. Hawker (see Day 12) buried over forty who were washed up within the parish boundaries. We toasted their souls in the fine Bush Inn, which Kate often visits, with claims to be one of the oldest pubs in the county. Dating back to the 13th century, it must stand a chance, especially as many ghosts have reportedly been seen wandering around the place, and who will testify to this claim.

Our hosts in 17th century farmhouse Little Bryaton could not have been more accommodating, and Jan cooked us a great and romantic Candlelit Dinner in the evening, of three courses 'plus cheese and coffee' during which the Bish started to quiz me about that Hawker chap. I reproached him, preferring to talk about the movement in Base Rate since we had last walked, and said he had to wait.

Day 12. My return to Bude, after some 50 odd years was only eight miles down the road, so to speak, but after a superb non-Candlelit breakfast, we headed back down towards the sea, and the smallest National Trust site in the whole wide world, namely 'Hawkers Hut'.

Having failed miserably on the health and safety front, the Bishop had appointed me as Head of Ecclesiastical Research, and when we got to said hut I was then able to relate the tale of the Reverend Robert Hawker, which I will have to keep as brief as possible, especially as he was one of life's true eccentrics. He had lived in Morwenstow as a child, and, having being ordained in 1831 he was more than chuffed when he was offered the rectorship of the parish church three years later. He served as vicar to the smugglers, wreckers and dissenters of the area for the next 40 years. He is known to have dressed up as a mermaid and danced along the beach. He excommunicated his cat for mousing on Sundays. He talked to the birds, invited cats into church, and he kept a huge pig as a pet.

As noted previously, he was concerned that bodies of drowned men received a Christian burial, and would scramble down to the beach, and carry back their bodies to the churchyard. His poem, Song of Western Men, became Cornwall's National Anthem, and he began the tradition of Harvest Festival in 1843.

At the hut, which he had constructed of driftwood, and is about the size of your average downstairs toilet, he spent much of his time contemplating, writing poetry and smoking opium. And then on his death bed, he converted to the Roman Catholic Church.

The views from the hut are awesome, and from where we

could see Lundy Island to our right, and what was probably Tintagel in the far distance to the south. How fulfilling would it have been if I could have written this book from that hut, which conveniently had a Wi-Fi connection. I told you he was eccentric! Not sure about the opium bit though, merlot on tap would have been fine for me.

It was tough going down to Bude, but we were sort of getting used to it, and having overspent in Morwenstow, the first thing we looked for, after finding what turned out to be our very average B&B, was a Bank. Bit like going back to work.

It's crude in Bude in the nude. Not that we did, it is an expression that has sort of stuck in my mind. On our travels it was the first of many touristy places we were to pass through, and one I left with little regret. Two, albeit fine beaches, a canal, the usual seaside shops and guest houses around a golf course is all I recall, save for the memories.

In life, you can look back and some, often inconsequential, things stick in your brain. It was 5 August 1962, when I was last in Bude, and only 11 years old. We had forsaken the austerity of the B&B in Ilfracombe and my parents had found us a farmhouse on the outskirts of Bude to stay for our week's holiday. As we pulled up to park on that day, the farmer's son, who we had played cricket with the day before, rushed up to us, and as we wound the window down, exclaimed "Marilyn Monroe has died". At the time, she was, in every quarter, a sex symbol and her death at such a tender age of 36 a complete surprise. The official cause of her death is recorded as a 'Barbiturate overdose'. Whilst I just love conspiracy stories, how can I possibly believe that the two Kennedy brothers, who were both allegedly bonking her at the time, allegedly had nothing to do with her death? Poor Norma Jean.

Ten years later to the very day, I got married.

Day 13. Bude to Crackington Haven. We continued in fine

weather the last 10 miles walking of the year, initially along low grassy cliffs and overlooking the surfers and superb beaches and views. Widecombe Bay was the highlight, but no pub. I do recall, and have a picture to prove it, passing a sign that said 'Crackington Haven 4¾ miles. It seemed like 43 miles, as when after every turning on this tough stretch, I longed to see the village, and when we eventually got there, boy was I tyred and exhausted. A good name or what for a garage specialising in such accessories methinks.

135 miles done, and 26,000 ft of ascent, and not a drop of rain in the four years.

Later in this year I had the holiday of a lifetime, first in Sydney, then New Zealand, then the Cook Islands. I hope you find the stories of my time in those countries, later in this book, a good read.

CHAPTER 6

2007
Crackington Haven to Trevone Bay

THIS YEAR saw the first iPhone go on sale. Poor Madeleine McCann disappeared, whilst John Inman, Anita Roddick and Alan Ball died.

Now I was never a great fan of Alan Ball, either as a player or manager (especially when at City) but my view changed when I saw him speak at a Sportsman's Dinner at Bolton Wanderers Burnden Park, now a retail park. He is a Farnworth lad, like my son. When he stood up to speak, being a smallish chap at five foot six, he did say "For those of you sitting at the back, I am standing up". He therefore immediately passed the 15 second rule, and another rule in life in that you should never be afraid to take the P155 out of yourself. His book was great too, and he tragically died in the middle of the night whilst trying to put out a fire in his back garden.

T'internet also overlooks that in this year I was made redundant for the second time in my life, and moved into the life of self-employment. It always tickles me that organisations give you money to go, and thank you, this time, Bolton Council. At least from now on I didn't have to look at the holiday list when arranging these annual sojourns.

Day 14. Whilst I haven't gone into the logistics of this kind of walking, I will do that later, but on this day in May I flew down to Exeter, where Colin picked me up in his brand new Renault and we headed off cross country back to Crackington Haven, and a tough 7 miles to Boscastle followed. The guide book says this section has the highest cliffs in Cornwall, and advises the walker to keep away from the high and sheer cliff edges…as if we wouldn't! As luck would have it, this was the first day of the whole walk that it rained, and, seemingly by way of protest, my waterproof which had gone unused for the previous 13 days, decided not to work. Thankfully as we approached Boscastle the sun came out, and the guide refers to its harbour as 'rugged cliffs enclosing a peaceful haven'. Tell that to the people who were there on 16 August 2004.

Whilst I have already written about the flood that destroyed Lynmouth with 34 fatalities, it is often recorded that, of the resident population of a thousand, and say an equal number of visitors, not one human life was lost that day in Boscastle, although two dogs were reported to have been washed out to sea.

I am indebted to chap called David Rowe who has written a superb account of what happened on that afternoon, after a sunny summer's day morning, when the skies darkened and there was a massive cloudburst and then a ferocious flood. He refers to 'The Magnificent Seven' – a team of helicopters from the Royal Navy, RAF and Coastguard who carried out what was seen to be the biggest peacetime rescue mainland Britain has ever known.

Walking round the village, three years later like we were, there was precious little evidence of the horrors of that afternoon. In the book there are some wonderful quotes, some from residents, which I will share now.

Aside from the weather forecast for the day being 'scattered showers, becoming heavy in the afternoon', we read:

"I clung onto the drainpipe. I thought I'm going to die and I think I swore. Loads";

"I opened a bottle of wine, and then I heard screams";

"My runner beans disappeared before my eyes" (love that one!);

"If we get out alive I'll never shout at the children again"....and finally,

"An eel tried to swim into my neighbour's house".

Our B&B was a little way up the valley and was hardly affected by the horrors that occurred below, although my initial opinion of our host was confirmed.

The planning process of distance walking can be challenging, in that inevitably after three or four days walking a car has to be at the end, to get you back to the start, where a car has been sitting for an equal period. For this reason, when I am booking, especially B&B's, I always try to speak to the owner, chat them up like you do, and explain the situation with regard to parking. Up to this juncture our hosts had been understanding and helpful, save for Mr Misery Guts brother here in Boscastle, who clearly knew as much about Customer Care as I do about fishing. He had no space for me to leave a car, and anyway there was the council Car Park nearby. And if any of you out there know anything about parking charges in this part of the world, they don't come cheap, especially in the tourist havens like Boscastle.

As it happened my plans changed, but in walking up to the house there must have been room for at least 6 cars, and yes, there was the sign 'Will all walkers please remove their boots before entering the porch'. Our welcome brought a whole new meaning to the word 'cold', as was the breakfast, but at least our dinner at a local pub was warm and friendly, and in teasing the waitress like you do about what the meal came with, I recall her saying "but I am not a potato person!".

Day 15. A moderate to severe day beckoned as 14 miles would take us to Port Isaac, via Tintagel. The first part typified the best of coastal walking, with headlands, springy turf, sandy bays, historic features and the inevitable steep valleys. At least the weather had improved, and we were soon in and out of Tintagel, where we did not linger, despite, with its derelict castle, 'fascinating' 14th century Old Post Office', and all the King Arthur baloney, it being one the most iconic visitor attractions in the south west. Why the haste, you may wonder.

I had been there before, the Saturday tourists were everywhere, like termites mingling on a vegetable patch, and at one stage we had to queue, yes queue, here on the South West Coastal Path, to get away from them as they made their way onto the island with its castle remains. I cracked a 'joke' with my friend by saying: 'The fattest knight at King Arthur's round table was Sir Cumference. He acquired his size from eating too much pi'. Not surprisingly I got no response back from him.

We were soon back solo on the Bish&Vic roadshow, as the scenery and weather got better, but nothing much better than having dropped down to Trebarwith Strand, where a pint of Tribute bitter was drunk and thoroughly enjoyed. Port Isaac bound, the top area of the village was in direct contrast to the lovely unspoilt harbour below where I experienced one of those iconic moments in time.

We knew our B&B was actually on the path itself on the way out and up from the harbour, and as I started the approach, a seemingly very nice lady approached me and enquired "Are you Mr Bullock?"

Now I know I have been on television (although I was only 12 years old at the time and had some hair and sideburns) and have been referred to by chums as "a famous walker and author", but here I was some 400 miles from home and someone recognised me. I thought I am going to milk this one til the bullocks come home, whilst my walking partner, being of a higher order, had that look of 'Do you not know who **I** am?'

Naturally there was a logical explanation. Said lady was our friendly landlady for the night, who was going out for the evening and was running late. Or, we were walking late. With loaded rucksacks, and clearly two men on a mission, she advised it wasn't a difficult task recognising us. She told us her house was the last one at the top of hill, the back door was open, we were in Room 3, and there were some cans in the fridge should we fancy a drink. And what would we like for breakfast? Now that's what I call Customer Service.

As we ambled up Rosscarrock Hill (true, but I may have added an 's') to our left was a detached building with signs in the window to the effect of 'Bog Off whilst there is filming going on'. It meant nothing to us at the time, and only later did I learn that we were in the fictional village of Portwenn and it was Doc Martin's building where he held surgery. Should you also be a fan, where we stayed is the extreme right semi-detached at the top of the hill in the distance on the opening credits.

First filmed there in 2004 there have been 54 episodes aired on ITV, the last one in 2015. Whilst not everyone's cup of tea, including the Bishop, I happen to love it, especially when I can relate to areas which we know and have walked around. Martin Clunes is a brilliant actor in my book, and who of you out there would not love him as your doctor? I know he can be a bit grumpy, but there is none of 'try these and if it doesn't work come back in two weeks' time'. You get an instant diagnostic of your problem, whatever that may be, and in an emergency he's your man. I recall an episode when someone was in serious danger and he was asked if said person would die, to which he retorted "Yes! One day, but maybe not today. Now get out of my way!"

He is also a great dog lover and is on record as saying that "a man is not a man without a dog". Despite loving dogs myself I am inclined to disagree, but he tells a great story, in that often in filming in Port Isaac, crowds invariably watch. In the inevitable breaks, he often goes over to talk to them, and is often drawn to people with dogs. And then some people without a dog borrow one from a friend, knowing that he would almost certainly go over to speak to them!

Day 16. Port Isaac remains one of the highlights of the walk. With its boats, nets and lobster pots, together with a fine restaurant, many of the streets have just enough room for one to thread between the buildings. A passage is superbly named Squeeze Belly Alley, where even stout pedestrians struggle to pass through. Nearby, a Land Rover once crashed into someone's roof. I was to return at another time, and couldn't get into the village as a man approached me with a clip board and told me they were filming. My hero was in the distance, but on this occasion I wasn't recognised. I didn't have a dog with me either.

After a fine breakfast we were off to Padstow, well almost, and whilst only 12 miles it had everything a walker could ask for (except no pub stop). To the idyllic Port Quinn it was a bit of a roller coaster, and energy sapping. To Polzeath it became more open and we certainly enjoyed The Rumps, and the outlook at Pentire Point. It then became a lot tamer, almost domesticated and continuing through some sand dunes, along the Camel Estuary towards a place called Rock, who should I see walking towards us but my present wife, Elaine. What a surprise that wasn't (mobile phones and all that) as, after all, it was all part of my cunning plan. We had a celebratory drink in a posh, probably too posh for walkers, establishment overlooking the fine estuary and Padstow. In case you were wondering, you can get a quite modest 3-bedroom property in Rock for about £600k on a good day. Our drinks were blooming expensive too.

With mobility now to hand with Elaine in the driving seat, I had booked us in at a 'place' overlooking Trevone Bay, on the other side of Padstow. I failed miserably. For marks out of ten I would be struggling to give it one, although the young lady who ran it, with her mother, seemed pleasant enough. More of which, later.

I like Christopher Richard 'Rick' Stein OBE. I admire his humility and modesty. What I know about cooking and food you could put on the back of my business card, but he is a star in my one eye. Strangely he took similar 'A' levels to me. He took History, Geography and English and I took History, Geography and French. He failed them all, and, to my mother's great chagrin I failed French. He went on to become a highly successful entrepreneur and I became a boring banker. At the last count he was worth, with his former wife, £32million and employs over 450 people in Padstow,

As part of the planning process I usually plan our year's walk in January. Taking account of the usual logistical issues, I knew that on the evening of Sunday 13 May we would be able to dine in Padstein (as it is often now known) and in one of Rick's four restaurants, all offering something different, but generally upmarket. I found one I liked, rang up, and the kind receptionist advised that she could only accommodate us at 8.00pm but no later. And that was in four month hence. Is that not indicative of something special, or what?

The three of us enjoyed our evening meal, which was good not great. But in the overall scheme of things it had been a superb day, and hopefully there would be many to follow.

Day 17. Despite stunning views, our room in the 'hotel' was truly awful and how could I forget that single cubicle shower, with grouting that varied between minging white, grey and black. I think the bed may have been new twenty years previous. The breakfast was of the type where the baked beans had taken on some form of epidemic and covered all before it, and under and over it. We checked out, despite having booked there for two nights. Thankfully I had a Plan B, with the 'B' standing, in this instance, for breakfast.

I can't remember when I last walked on a Monday, this being 13 May. Come to think of it I don't recall the last time I worked on a Monday either. Indeed, I once worked with someone in the Bank who said he hated Mondays, because it was back to work after the weekend. I told him he must hate a seventh of his life, and needed to get a grip. He was soon transferred to Grimsby, and that was the last I heard of him.

A fine day beckoned and this was to be a gentle stroll up and round Padstow Bay, finishing up 6 miles later at Trevone Bay. As we were being picked up by MB Taxis we didn't have to carry our hefty rucksacks, and it was amazing what a difference it made. It was almost like being naked, although we didn't get as far as Booby's Bay that day.

177 miles completed. Over a quarter of the walk conquered. It was all downhill now down to Land's End.

CHAPTER 7

2008
Trevone Bay to Portreath

BARACK OBAMA WAS ELECTED, the QE2 was retired from service and in the Olympics in Beijing, Usain Bolt beat the world records in winning both the 100 and 200 metres. Paul Newman, Charlton Heston and Bo Diddley died, as did that fine climber Edmund Hilary. Now there was a man who knew a challenge when he saw one.

My first year's trading as a Self-Employed Business Adviser, saw me return Sales of a staggering £4442 and a Loss before drawings of £284. I told Bish that if things didn't get better we would be camping en route the year following. He said he would pray for me. I said I should have done a Business Plan.

Sheik Mansour bought my beloved Manchester City, and overnight we became the richest football club in the world. What a difference a day makes eh? That big project began, whilst this one just sort of rambled on.

Research revealed that this stretch would be hard work, with the odd highlight and a few 'downlights' for want of a better word. We were to reach Portreath, some 50 miles away, and our hosts there Mr and Mrs Helpful, were exactly that.

Day 18. The walk from Trevone Bay to Treyarnon Bay saw us idling along some superb sandy beaches, popular with those surfing characters, and with the tide out, we were able to walk across at ease. It's funny but by doing this it always seems like you are cheating. More excitement followed as we got a taxi back to Padstow, where we were staying at the Woodlands Country House. This was my Plan B, as recently referred to, and is run by the eccentric but highly likeable Hugo Woolley.

Breakfast, to a distance walker, is important as it sets the standard for the day. I believe in starting the day with a positive. My first job now, every morning, is invariably to pick up dog poo in a plastic bag. After that, things can only get better, as the song goes. Hugo is spot on, in what he said to me, in that many such establishments in the country are beautifully decorated, comfortable, have great service and food awards for lunch and dinner, but breakfast is usually of secondary importance and can be a disaster.

Our breakfast, as you would expect as I have set the scene, was brilliant. Interestingly, no tea bags, but proper tea, and you get used to using a strainer. Hugo has written a brilliant book, imaginatively called Breakfast, which you can get from Amazon, for £7.74.

Day 19. This was to see a 13 mile section to Newquay, generally, and thankfully along high flat-topped cliffs, and a few headlands. My ideal and favourite walking, occasionally we had to dip down to the sea like at Mawgan Porth, and yes, you are getting the hang of this, for a refreshing pint.

I must mention Bedruthan Steps, volcanic rock stacks, which I first visited all those years ago as a little bullock. Supposedly named after a Cornish giant, he used the steps as stepping stones across the bay. And if you fancy a dip in the sea there, forget it. So dangerous, **Swimming is banned.** We soon encountered a snake on the path, sliding along without a care in the world. It told us about a new restaurant, at

Watergate Bay a bit further along, and which Richard Nixon had visited.

Called Fifteen Cornwall, it has a superb setting overlooking the wide expanse of beach. The menu looked pretty interesting too. With Jamie Oliver input, it is a community type operation, with profits going to a local charity, the Cornwall Food Foundation. Unfortunately we had to get to Newquay and couldn't linger, and as we climbed the steps off Porth Beach, a different world opened out.

It well known that in this country there are two Newquays, this one and one in Wales. However, there are clearly two Newquays in Cornwall.

According to the county's tourist board it is one of the nation's favourite seaside towns, where the whole family can relax and enjoy a proper (?) holiday – toes in the sand, ice cream in hand. It manages to be trendy but remains a great family resort, with seven beaches all within easy reach. There are lots to do for night owls, who like to live it up when the sun goes down.

Then there's the grotty Newquay we walked into, along littered streets, past tacky looking gift shops, old Victorian like hotels, and of the population of some twenty thousand, half of them seemed to be surfers. Now also a magnet for stag and hen parties, thanks to the airport just up the coast, I bet the aforementioned night owls were happy sitting up in the safety of the trees, looking down on puking grooms and braying brides. To cap it all, there was our evening's, and I use the word loosely, 'accommodation'.

The best product or service in the world still has to be sold. The worst product or service in the world can still have the best website, and feature on Google Page One. I can't recall what took me to choosing this one in Newquay, but clearly it put into doubt my diabolical surfing skills. En suite is so important, yet all we had was a grotty corner sink with no towel. It had more teddy bears all over the room than you could find in Mothercare. And when the Bish found the bathroom, there was a lady's bra and knickers on the floor. To his eternal credit, and being part of his nature, he forgave me for this choice, and found a superb place for our evening meal.

Day 20. The best thing about Newquay is the way out, and confusingly there are four exit routes for us walkers, all depending on the tide and time of day, the month, the weather, the sea conditions and what you had for breakfast (oh yes, that was crap too!) Thankfully we found the easiest and quickest route, fighting through a few sand dunes, and we were on our way to Perranporth some 12 miles away. As the tide was out we were able to nip across Porth Joke (not joking), avoid being shot at the Ministry of Defence site at Penhale Sands, and in no time at all we were on the northern edge of Perran Beach, which led all the way to our day's destination. A straight 3 mile stretch along the sands saw me writing many messages of love and devotion to my current wife with my stick in the sand, whilst the Bishop was in silent prayer that, at least, our evening base couldn't be as bad as our previous evening.

Alleluja!! Well almost. You would have thought by now I would have got the hang of the booking process, so how come I chose a gay friendly country house on the top of a hill, a mile out of the town. Thankfully we had separate beds, there was a bath, everything was impeccable and the perfect ending to a great day.

Day 21. Our last day of this year, another 12 mile stroll in the country (13 to be exact because of our start point) to Portreath, mainly flat, but with still over 2,000ft of climbing, we were into mining country, and in this area mainly tin and copper, prominent in the 18th and 19th century. A few derelict buildings remain, but most were destroyed by the elements or by man. Allegedly we were in Poldark country, but as expected the series was filmed all over the county. A fine man, of course, with a fine Christian name, I can readily recall the mid 1970's when the series became compulsive viewing early on Sunday evenings. The more recent retake seemed to be more about his hairy chest than anything else.

The port at Portreath served the local mining activities, but is now another perhaps non-chocolate box seaside town, but a lovely couple there looked after two middle aged, ex bankers with great kindness.

It was a long journey home on the Sunday, with a diversion off the M6 at Stoke, and I nearly missed seeing Willie Nelson at the Apollo in Manchester. He did play one of my all-time favourite songs "Always on my Mind" but seemed more intent in throwing his hat (or hats as was the case) into the audience after every song. He was 75 at the time, and is still performing I believe.

214 miles gone, a third of the way, and naturally greater walking experiences to come.

CHAPTER 8

2009
Portreath to Land's End

AN INTERESTING, but all round great year. The last Woolworth's branch closed. There used to be 813 of them, and they had over 27,000 employees, of which I was once one, albeit in the short period of 8 months from August 1972. With the grand title of Trainee Manager, the staff referred to people like me as being a 'Floor Walker'. In the Bolton branch I learnt how to sweep floors, catch mice (there were hundreds in the store) cut the glass that divided the items on the counters, and dream of not working on a Saturday, as I was missing out on trips to Maine Road to watch my beloved team.

Base rate was reduced to 1.50% and then to 0.50%. Serious bad news for the old folk who saved up for their retirement. Serious good news for many others, including my sons.

The now late great Terry Wogan presented his last morning breakfast show, and early morning radio has never been the same since. Clement Freud, Danny La Rue and Bobby Robson all died.

And I went to prison.

The walk was settling into a pattern, in that it would generally revolve around the second weekend in May. My favourite month, by a country mile, the days are generally long, the weather good (fact) there are masses of beautiful flowers, there are few people about, and booking accommodation generally not a problem.

The driving inevitably increased the further down the peninsula, and the journey to Portreath was 355 miles. With new or little listened to cd's in my faithful Bora, I would set off at about 4am, thereby missing out the hiatus of the M6/M5 around Spaghetti Junction, but it did get a bit busy around Bristol. Leaving the M5 around Exeter, the A30 took me westwards, and this year my journey took about 7½ hours....all to walk 40 odd miles. Whose idea was this, by the way?

However, this was a special year, in that we would reach Land's End, but alas, nowhere near half way along the Path.

Day 22. I got to know our hosts at the Cliff House, Mr and Mrs Helpful quite well, as I stayed there at the completion of 2008, and again at the start of 2009. Mrs Helpful (Gillian) was a superb cook, whilst her husband readily took up the role of looking after our cars, despite there only being two parking spaces outside, and ferrying us around. Take note the Misery Guts.

This day was to see us head for Hayle, some 13 miles away. Of moderate variety, walking on the high level cliffs continued to please me, as did seeing the seals at Navas point. The only seal I had seen before was a Company Seal, used for 'legalising any contract entered into by a company' in case you are the least bit interested, but now long since abolished. Walking through sand dunes, along the sand, and pavement, characterised the second half of the day, as the delights of Hayle beckoned.

Day 23. It is hard to be kind about Hayle, and as I spoke to Elaine on the mobile, she asked where I was and I told her I was outside Jewsons, with fantastic views of an industrial estate, coal yards and a power station. Undoubtedly a low point of this northern coast of Cornwall, at least we had St Ives (famous for its pilchards) not far away, as we headed for an evening's overnight stay at Gurnards Head Hotel.

A major downer in distance walking, as I have said, is that it often becomes a bit like a route march, and this was quite a long day, and not helped by us learning of a diversion ahead due to a rock fall. The tourist board rave about the town in a similar way they do about Newquay, but in this case they seemed to have got it right. It had everything, from a unique setting, a working harbour, great golden sands, crystal blue waters, cobbled streets, art galleries, if you are into that sort of thing, and, how could I forget, a great Village Hall where the ladies of the local WI were serving morning drinks and cakes, which we thoroughly enjoyed.

One of them asked us if we were walkers, which was a bit like asking if you had black coffee without milk. Bish told them about our pilgrimage, and that I was a famous author and walker, and thinking we were joking, the conversation sort of died an immediate death as she seemed anxious to serve a more a normal type of customer.

Unfortunately, we had no time to linger in this great location, also known to be the best place in the country to watch the migration of sea birds, and as the weather began to threaten, Bish slipped badly on the path to Clodgy Point (clodgy is Cornish for leper, by the way). Fortunately he fell on the pasty resting happily in his pocket, so no injury, other than to the poor pasty, of course.

This was a very remote and wild area, and the diversion took us into Zennor, the first and probably best inland village we had come across. It's famous, not only for having once been the home of D H Lawrence, but a carving of the famed 'Mermaid Chair' in the church, she having a mirror in one hand and a comb in the other. Naturally we missed it, but I didn't miss having a pint of Mermaid in the local Tinners Arms.

Seemingly in the middle of nowhere, with remoteness abounding, and the sea not in sight, as we turned into yet another field, there it was, with its name on the roof, the Gurnard's Head Hotel. Day done, another 12 miles ticked off.

Day 24. A special day in many ways, it was bright but cold in this exposed area. We were Land's End bound, and wouldn't have to pay the £4 parking charge either when we got there.

It was a bright windy day, with it being very remote and exposed, it had it all. There were some serious scrambles, and stark cliffs, rocky pinnacles, and small coves to negotiate. Part of this area was used as a training area for commandos in World War Two.

And when you think it couldn't get much better it did, as we approached the tin mines of Pendeen, with some engine houses still intact, and with old chimneys on the horizon L S Lowry would have loved it here. In many ways it was sad to walk through all the dereliction and heaps of shale, although it did remind me of the time I worked in Wigan.

We walked out to the Cape Cornwall, crowned with a tall chimney standing in isolation; it misses out by only 1,000 yards in being the most westernmost point in England to Land's End, which we could see in the distance. Peaceful, but at the same time wild, we sat there for a few minutes to take it all in, whilst Bish divulged the last bits of the pasty he had found in his pocket.

Pasties have long been associated with Cornwall; although the word 'pasty' apparently derives from Medieval French would you believe, going back as far as the 14th century. It became popular around here especially when the miners adopted it in view of its unique shape, forming a complete meal that could be easily eaten without cutlery. In the mines its dense folded pastry could stay warm for hours, and if it did get cold it could be easily warmed over a candle. Indeed, as the miner would probably have dirty hands, the thick edge of the pasty would be cast aside.

Now regarded as the national dish of the county, there is the Cornish Pasty Association that keeps an eye on things, and determines the factors that go into it being a genuine Cornish pasty. They can fall back too on the EU for a recognised framework that gives legal protection for named regional food products to combat imitation. Enter also the Melton Mowbray Pork Pie.

Inevitably as we progressed around this great county, our day would invariably start with us seeking out the local pasty shop in the morning for our lunchtime stop, and chose from the large variety on offer, some of which would have been unheard of in the olden days. It seemed boring to choose the original ones (meat and potato) when you could have lamb tikka, chicken and tarragon, corned beef and baked beans, cheese, pickle and onions whatever. But as I often say, it's nice to have options, and on this particular day there was only one....to reach Land's End.

Which we did, stopping off at the village of Sennon Cove. Clearly this is a serious spot for surfers, who on this day seemed to be outnumbered by warning signs, instructions, life-guards and ambulances. Linger not, it seemed to have the widest path to date as we approached Land's End, the Skegness of the west coast of England.

I knew I would be disappointed, as I had been there before, but how we have ruined such an iconic spot in our country. I know I could be accused of being biased but who would put a hotel, pub, visitor centre, cafes, 4d film experiences, theme park, children's 'farms', shopping malls, slot machines,' oh' I could go on, at the likes of Cheddar Gorge, Malham Cove, the Giants Causeway, the Needles, Seven Sisters Cliffs, High Cup

Nick etc. Only someone like entrepreneur Peter de Savary, who outbid the National Trust in 1987, in paying £7million for it, and is largely responsible for how it looks today. I wish he had stuck with football. He was Chairman of Millwall FC. He could have used that money to buy an average left back, and that would have left this great landmark back where it should have been...with the National Trust, who seem to know about how to look after such significant landmarks.

Every cloud has a silver lining, not that there was one in the sky as we approached the notorious 'First and Last House in England' And who should be there, the one and only lady from MB Taxis, who had flown into Newquay airport, where she was met by Mr Helpful from the B&B in Portreath, and whose Christian name I now know as being Extremely, who took her back to Portreath to pick up my car, and here she was, not only in body and mind, but as importantly clutching a chilled bottle of Veuve Champagne for her to share and celebrate with two weary ex bankers cum clergymen as a result of their epic 257 mile adventure, which had only taken a mere 7 years. As they say, if something is worth doing, it is worth savouring.

A few days later, Elaine and I flew to the Stupid Isles, for a short break, in what can only be described as a very small, 8 seater plane. We were weighed before embarking, for balancing purposes. Now more usually called the Scilly Isles, there are over a hundred of them, although only five inhabited. Favourite place of the late Harold Wilson, we visited his grave in a small churchyard on the island of St Mary's. Somehow I can't see 'President' Blair being buried in somewhere so humble can you?

A great place, however, renowned for its incredibly mild temperature and palm trees my lasting memory of the place was that we couldn't find anywhere nice to eat, and twitchers......well they were everywhere....and easily seemed to outnumber the birds themselves.

CHAPTER 9

2010
Land's End to Loe Bar

THIS YEAR, from Land's End to the Lizard, was pretty straightforward and easy to plan. I would fly down to Newquay, Bish would pick me up and we would drive to the Lizard where he would leave his car. Taxi to Land's End, and four days walk back to the Lizard. Q.E.D.

My time in prison was having a dramatic impact on my Profit and Loss Account, to the effect that HMR&C loved it too, by sending me nasty bills. To clarify, in 2009 the Lovely Linda from Bolton Council asked me to lead a project which was aimed at getting local offenders who were ready for release from prison, and those already out, usually on probation, employment. The whole issue invariably got down to re-offending, in that if they didn't get work, they often slipped back into their old ways, and soon ended up back in prison.

As a result I spent quite a lot of time in the nick. Certainly an eye opener the highlight was usually being actively frisked on entry by a lady prison officer. After a while I got used to the life, and I learnt a lot about the criminal world, and one lad often boasted how easy it was to get drugs in prison. Indeed, about 80% of the prisoners I counselled and helped, their offence was invariably drugs related in some way. I did, however, struggle with the sex offenders, although had to be professional as best I could.

I have often said that the best thing, if you have to go to hospital, is being able to walk out. The same could also be said after a day in prison. As for the role, it is pleasing to reveal we met our targets, and then, as was the norm the funding ran out. However, looking back, banking certainly was a lot easier.

In this year there was the BP Oil spill in the Gulf of Mexico, and there was the Icelandic volcanic eruption which created havoc in the airways, there being a great conspiracy there if you google it. Apple announced that they had sold 3m iPads in the first 80 days of release, and the word 'app' was introduced into our vocabulary. Alex Higgins died, as also did Norman Wisdom and Michael Foot.

As you may guess I left Land's End with few regrets. Then as I write this I think of people, some of sound mind and character, who walk there from John o' Groats, a modest 874 miles. I can't imagine how they feel when they reach Land's End. To them it must be the best place in the universe, equivalent to say when I saw the sun rising over Machu Picchu, the Border Hotel at Kirk Yetholm as we finished the Pennine Way, or my first visit to the Etihad Stadium in Manchester. Memories, and precious ones too.

Day 25. As we had a late start, this was a short 5 miles from Land's End to Porthcurno. Whilst to date there had been some memorable moments, such as Hartland Quay, Clovelly, Padstein, the amble along Perran Beach, and the harbour at St Ives, we had reached a turning point for the whole walk. It was like the volume had been turned up. Gone were the wild winds, occasional remote stretches and bleakness, mining remains and those super active surfers.

The crowds were now behind us, and the cliffs simply awesome. Completely different to what had gone before, the granite stumps (for want of better terminology) looked like big fat stalagmites rising directly out of the sea. There were little offshore islands, the domain of gulls, who were extremely territorial and warded off other birds who dared to try and land there. It was relatively easy walking, leaving the cliff tops only occasionally to descend into superb coves, notably the one at Porthgwarra.

We completed the walk far too quickly, and for me this was probably the most memorable stretch of the whole SWCP. We soon arrived at the open air Minack Theatre, constructed above a gully with a rocky outcrop jutting into the sea. It was the brainchild of Rowena Cade, who spent over 50 years of her life building its terraces and stage into the rock face, in true Greek/Roman style all by herself with the help only of her gardener. The first production was held in 1932 and there is now a full programme of events every year from Easter to September, with an audience of up to 750 people. As luck would have it, it had closed for visitors for the day, and I already knew there was no play for us to watch. And we didn't see any of it either from the outside, as none of it is visible landside.

Here in Porthcurno, with a superb beach and with a history revolving around early wireless communications, saw us dine in a very average pub, on what was to be a dramatic night in the country's history, with half the population glued to their television sets up until mid-night at least. Bish and I had more important things to discuss rather than the implications of the General Election that night and the resulting hung parliament. My pleasure at Labour losing out seemed to put Mr B&B ill at ease as he quickly showed us the door the following morning, as another great day beckoned. Think he was called Gordon, and he appeared to be thoroughly Browned off.

Day 26. It was about 13 miles to Penzance, described in my guide as strenuous. For most of it I would have called it glorious. The westerly wind was now behind us, and the sun in front of us. The wildlife loved it too, and we passed bluebell fields, and arum lilies squashed between rocky outcrops. Mainly walking on the cliffs, the downward steps invariably brought us into superb little coves like at Penberth. Superb, also in the fact that if you drove down to them you couldn't park anyway and look round, so they remained the preserve of the fishing boats and those very special people…coastal path walkers.

10 miles later we reached Mousehole, which all the guide books explain is pronounced 'Mowzul'. This was my second visit to this pleasant harbour village. The first time, many moons ago, we couldn't get anywhere near it because 'Air Miles Andy' was visiting. And I used to think so highly of him when he went to fight in the Falklands.

Whilst Bish looked round the village, which the Spanish totally destroyed in 1595, I took sanctuary in the imaginatively named Ship Inn (2), and chatting to an old geezer at the bar whilst I ordered my glass of coke, as if you believe that one. I asked him what he thought of the election result. "What election?" came the reply, as he looked down and continued to carefully study his beer mat.

The final three miles into Penzance, via Newlyn, are best described as average, with the town's status being enhanced by it having the last pilchard works in the county. Fast forward six years, and which town will claim to have the last HSBC branch in Cornwall?

Day 27. We had now walked 275 miles, and the following 14 miles would take us to one of my favourite places in the county, if not the country, that being Porthleven. Sorry, but my memories of Penzance, the largest place we had come across since Newquay, are completely blank although I am sure Tourist Cornwall will rave about it if you visit t'internet.

An unexciting walk along the bay to Marazion was dominated by views of the iconic St Michael's Mount which has had many guises since the 12th century when it was a Priory, soon to be a fortress, then a port for exporting tin and copper, and now the good old National Trust is its custodian. Reached by ferry, or foot when the tide is out, I have failed on at least three occasions now to visit it, but I can always resort to YouTube should the mood take me.

The path takes you through the middle of the town, where there was a little market selling Greenwood Penny Christmas Trees, and as we resumed towards the sea past the local cemetery, Bish exclaimed, "Is that not Darth Vader?" as he espied a walker not too far ahead. Dressed totally in black, as you expect our Jedi Knight to be attired, he seemed to be carrying the weight of the world on his shoulders, or at least 3 stones in his black rucksack, as he staggered along the path with two walking poles. No sooner as I uttered in reply to my learned superior "Let the force be with you", our Galactic warrior disappeared and was no longer to be seen.

Views of the Lizard now dominated the headland, and as we whizzed past Praa Sands with its grotty looking pub and seemingly enormous holiday park, my love affair with this south coast dwindled as the going got a bit tough, but the sight of the harbour at Porthleven changed all this and it was good to be back again here following my first visit, as a tourist, back in 2001. Then we had called in early morning to have a look round, stayed all day, and returned in the evening for a superb meal.

We have all done it, and I would be surprised if you hadn't too, often wondered, if there were no boundaries, work or family ties, where would you live in the country. I would like to think I have travelled around this wonderful island we live in, but if I had the choice, it would be Porthleven every time.

To me the place has everything. Although a tourist location, it is not in your face, if that makes sense. It exudes charm and tradition. It has what is arguably the best harbour in the county, and a working one too. Small fishing boats land their catch there, much of which is sold to the local restaurants. There are well preserved historic buildings, and delightful looking fisherman's cottages. The climate is mild, and benefits due to the warm waters of the Gulf Stream. That's why it has palm trees. The shops are varied and interesting. You couldn't buy a bucket and spade there if you tried. I did buy my first 'Man Bag' in one of them. There are loads of places to walk nearby and great beaches either side of the harbour, where you can also take boat trips from. There are many great places to eat and drink, and Mr Stein has one now. I could go on, and best shut up now, and let you find out for yourself one day. You won't be disappointed.

The town is also famous in that the Dam Busters VC Guy Gibson spent a great deal of his boyhood there, and in fact I found the street named after him. My father-in-law, Les Chester, served under him in the Second World War, and I have written his story which you will find later in this book.

That evening we ate at the superb Kota Restaurant. The Bishop chose a fish called John Dory, whilst I enjoyed a steak called T Bone. A fine Chilean Merlot was enjoyed, and as had become the norm, we didn't talk about banking.

We had a nightcap in the Ship Inn (3) overlooking the harbour and the sea, and toasted this iconic part of the country. On the way back we passed a shop, which had the following in its window, simply named 'The Weather Prayer'

> *Our father which art in Porthleven*
> *Fed up be thy name*
> *The rain has come*
> *Thy will be as wet in Helston*
> *As it is in Porthleven*
> *Give us an umbrella, for our daily soak*
> *And forgive us our daily moans*
> *As we forgive those who moan to us*

And lead us not into depression
But deliver us a pizza
For, Cornwall is the kingdom
The pasties and the cream
For ever and ever
Amen

All credit to the writer, Belinda Higgs.

Day 28. This day was to be a straightforward 12 mile walk to the Lizard, which we discussed in our friendly B&B over our traditional Full English (no mushrooms for me) when who should walk into the room but.......the one and only Darth Vader!

Naturally I soon engaged him in conversation as a fellow walker, and discovered he was actually a normal 'homo sapiens' called John, who lived in that London. He was having 'early life crisis' in that having left his wife, and resigning from his job in insurance, he sold his house and decided, before starting afresh, to walk from Land's End to John O'Groats, and all for charity. His previous walking experience had been to walk from his front door to his car every morning. He had soon worked out that he was seriously overloaded, and was leaving half his stuff at this establishment, otherwise he realised he may not make it down the driveway.

Having exchanged numbers, I was to meet up with him again a month later on one of the best (there has to be one) stretches of the Pennine Way from Malham to Horton in Ribblesdale. We shared experiences, like you do, and whilst I occasionally followed his progress via his blog, I know he completed the walk, and much to his credit too.

Reluctantly leaving Porthleven, being on a mission myself we soon reached Loe Bar. This is where a short sand bar separates a fresh water lake from the sea, and unfortunately many ships have come to grief here, most notably a frigate named Anson in 1807, where 100 lives were lost.

Soon after, my mobile rang. In comparison my grief was probably inconsequential, but an incident involving my ageing mother led me choosing to cut short the day and arrange to get home which I did. Bish was very understanding, thankfully.

CHAPTER 10

2011
Loe Bar to Helford

A LANDMARK YEAR, I reached 60 and naturally partied through the night. We were soon off on our travels, and back to New Zealand. You can read all about it later in this book, should you wish.

There were other significant events in the year. We beat the Aussies at cricket to win The Ashes. The cheque guarantee card was abandoned after 40 years. City won the FA Cup, our first major honour for 35 years, if you discount our magnificent victory against the mighty Gillingham in the Third Division Play-off final in 1999. We lost the great actor Pete Postlethwaite, Gerry Rafferty (Baker Street still one of my favourite tracks) and Bolton's own legend Nat Lofthouse. Gary Speed committed suicide, in circumstances I still feel are very strange.

Our trek was to see us round the Lizard, ending up at Helford. A challenging logistical exercise, we needed two cars, and I hired one after flying down to Newquay. Only two and a half days walking, but by far the most expensive of the whole walk.

Day 29. An easy stroll down to Mullion Cove was about 6

miles, and saw us challenged by finding the start point where we had finished in 2010. In true style I was able to locate a pub first, and yes, it was called the Ship Inn (4) before resuming along a very pleasant coastline soon reaching Gunwalloe Church, which is almost on the beach. There was a stone sculpture of a man with a stick in the graveyard, which spookily looked like Bish, but I daren't say. He had said he had always wished to have worked so close to the sea, but the nearest he ever got was the pier at Wigan.

BISH IN
A GRAVE
MOOD

As often, throughout the walk, there would be a bench overlooking the sea, dedicated to someone who was no longer with us. The plaque usually said something uninspiring like 'To Fred, who loved this view'. As we approached the delightful Polhu Cove, there was a City Blue bench, with plaque dedicated to Liz Rudd, with the following statement:

> "If ever our souls part to say goodbye
> meet me there, where the sea meets the sky;
> lost, but finally free."

Day 30. As days go, this was to be a pretty tough one from Mullion Cove to Coverack, 17 miles and some 2,600 ft of ascent. We also had a bit of driving, and had to get a car to Helford where we were to finish the following day. We had stayed in Mullion, a very pleasant village, but having had to leave the hire car in the public car park there, I was gutted to discover someone had clearly driven into the back of it. Nothing serious, but clearly noticeable, it wasn't the best start to the day.

The Bishop advised that in his early days of car ownership that wouldn't have happened because cars had bumpers. I retorted that my first car, a mini, didn't have them, but came instead with a big debt.

I recall when I had picked it up from the airport, they had asked me if, for an additional £12 I wanted the full insurance package, whatever that was. The nice lad would have done a fine job for the Bank selling PPI (yes, we all had to do it) but I took the view I wouldn't be doing many miles, and this was, indeed, a very nice part of the world.

In returning the car I naturally pointed out the damage. Same lad said "Oh that's not so bad, we'll let you know the repair bill". He didn't, of course, as he had my card details and a week later a debit appeared on my account of £322 (!) to which I had no recourse. Added to the £70 hire charge, that totalled £392. Can't you tell I used to work with figures? And more so, I only did 84 miles in the car, which worked out at £4.66 a mile. Insurance can pay, we all know that, but needless to say I wasn't to hire a car again.

It was not the clearest of days as we made our way toward the Lizard Point, as we passed Kynance Cove, a place with incredibly sad memories. My last visit there in 2003, saw Elaine and I sitting peacefully on the cliff top on a brilliant day, when soon a helicopter came over, and hovered for a long time over a prominent rock in the Bay. There was a lot of activity, but when we returned to our car later, there was an elderly man nearby lying face down on the grass sobbing his heart out. A coastguard approached us and advised us that said gentleman had just lost a close relative who had died when he fell off the rock into the sea, hence the helicopter. He couldn't be comforted in any way, but that tragic image has obviously stayed with me ever since.

Lizard Point is the most southerly point we would reach, and is like a breath of fresh air after its most westerly counterpart, Land's End. It is uncomplicated and natural; with superb views and an iconic lighthouse, with its beam being able to be seen from a distance of 21 miles. I don't recall the shop where Bish spotted a slate lampstand, but he was clearly taken by it as a present for his good lady. This slate, more properly known as serpentine, is unique to the Lizard, and there are only two pubs in the whole area that have serpentine beer-pump handles. In view of limited opening hours, Bish had only this chance of purchase, which meant that he had to carry it in his rucksack, which already weighed a ton, for the next two days.

Thankfully, we were able to get to Cadgwith before closing time of 3.00pm. Naturally I didn't want a drink, but my quest for serpentine beer-pump handles had begun in earnest. A superb working harbour with crab and lobster boats, every villager seemed to have a vessel on the beach. A gem of a place, it is many people's idea of a proper Cornish fishing village.

There followed a section of cliffs and coves, being sheltered from the prevailing south westerly winds, which after what had gone before was pleasingly quiet and remote. We still had some distance to cover when Bish suddenly exhorted "I've lost my phone!" After the usual investigation and interrogation we were left with no alternative but to turn back and look for it. Thankfully, and we both agreed that the Boss must have been looking down on us and helping us with the search, in less than a few hundred yards I found it resting peacefully by the path, adjacent to some fresh sheep dung. At least my promotion to a larger diocese was now in the offing.

Unusually passing by wild horses and ponies roaming around Beagles Point, with no further incidents in an action packed day, we hit Coverack. Overlooking a sand and shingle bay, it is one of many Cornish villages where smuggling once supplemented the fishing industry, clearly to evade import tax. The story goes that one local smuggler is said to have worked in league with his wife, who would peg a red shirt on the washing line when it was safe for him to come ashore with his contraband. Believe it or not, I was told, said individual was called Wayne.

Day 31. It was to be an easier 13 mile day to Helford, and journey's end for another year. A special day was soon to unfold.

The night previous, with a highly forgettable meal in a long forgotten venue, we had agreed that every day there should be a highpoint and low point. Certainly the dents in the hire car left me well and truly miffed, but I just loved Cadgwith and wished we could have stayed there longer.

We continued to be sheltered away from the prevailing winds, and there were several inland stretches where we had to walk round former quarries, but, in no time at all we reached Porthallow (locally known as Pr'alla) conveniently at lunchtime. Here we had the choice between the 'charming' Fat Apples café and the imaginatively named Five Pilchards pub. Naturally I preferred the former, and if you believe that.....

Of more significance, however, was that having completed 315 miles we were now, after a mere 9 years, at the half way point of the walk, and there was a marker on the beach to prove it. You may recall that thousands of individuals walk the Path every year, and amazingly, both whilst walking, or wherever we had stayed, we had not met one single person who was actually doing it. Enter Dolly, who after kindly taking a photo of us at said marker, joined us for a drink in the pub. And would you believe, it **did** have serpentine beer pump handles!

Of Dutch origin, she worked in local government in Holland, and was doing the walk, like us in annual stretches, but in no particular order. We exchanged email addresses, like you do, and as Bish fancied another cider, she left for Helford and we said we would see her later. We didn't, nor did she ever reply to my subsequent email. And in case you're wondering, there is no Darth Vader II story to follow here.

It was a pleasing, although not dramatic walk northwards to Nare Point and then westwards towards Gillan Greek. It was low tide, but we didn't fancy the wade across, and two miles later along the creek we arrived at the superb setting with church at St Anthony-in-Meneage, being one of the earliest Christian sites in Cornwall. Bish was well pleased to be there, as I was to be, an hour later when we arrived at Helford. The bashed hire car was still there, and it was back to The Lizard, and a final night in The Caerthillion. In the local pub, I broke my usual rule, when I approached a lady who had not one, but two bearded collies. We shared stories about this brilliant breed, as I was soon to acquire my third, Rosie, who was to feature later on the walk. Watch this space.

The high point of the day was clearly to have reached the half way point, and Bish, quite rightly saw the low point, in that after a great three days, our travels had ended for another year.

Culbone Church
Pulpit time for Bish

North towards Hartland Point
Now that was tough going

Bedruthan Steps
Not a giant sight

Perran Beach
That's what I call a beach!

Cape Cornwall
An iconic landmark

Land's End
Not even half way

Porthleven
My favourite place by a country mile

The Lizard
Bish goes serpentine shopping

CHAPTER 11

2012
Helford to Charlestown

WHAT A GREAT YEAR, with a sporting event far more significant than anything seen in the Summer Olympics in that London.

It all happened at 4:53.22 pm on Sunday 13 May, when Aguerooooooooooooooooooo scored that goal against QPR that gave my beloved City their first title for 44 years and sent me into a state of uncontrolled bouncing orgasmic delight, and in jumping up hit my flat head on the wooden beam above me, sending my blue blood all over the place. Our Premier League dreams had come true in blue, and all credit to Sky's Martin Tyler, seeming as thrilled as us all, in saying "I swear you will never see anything like this again, so watch it, drink it in..." And I haven't, although I may have had a drink or two soon after. Clearly not there myself, I know people who were, and to a man they still have difficulty in describing their feelings of what it was like, the best being that it was like 'an out of body experience'. My own similar experience was in New Zealand, although in completely different circumstances, and you can read about it in one of stories later in this book.

This year we lost Robin Gibb and Whitney Houston, who drowned in the bath and Neil Armstrong, allegedly the first man to walk on the moon, although he didn't like to talk about it all that much afterwards.

We needed to get some miles under our belt if we were to finish the walk this decade, and these four days saw us walk 45 miles to Charlestown, just down from St Austell.

Day 32. From Helford Passage to Falmouth is described as a moderate 10 miles, with little civilisation in between, and precious little to report. It was a dull day, and the only person we met was an old chap walking his dog, who asked us what we were up to, and suggested a short cut if we wanted to get to Falmouth a bit quicker. Naturally, being men of the cloth, we kept to the official route, and as we trundled on, we discussed what kind of employment the dog walker could have been in. Bish opined that he was probably in the legal profession. "No way", I replied, "he surely must have been a *Path*ologist!"

Day 33. Falmouth, with the largest natural harbour in Cornwall, had everything a visitor could want, including some attractive old pubs, but was not touristy. We were, however, two men on a mission, and it was a full day, with it being 14 miles to Portloe. A new challenge now entered our lives for the first time….catching a ferry. The alternative walk round the estuary was not appropriate as we did not have two days to spare, and much to the Bishop's chagrin there were two ferries in succession, the first to St Mawes (a biddies' retreat apparently but an extremely pleasant location) and then on to a place called Place, with the latter ferry being not much bigger than your average rowing boat. The only place in Place seemed to be Place House, a nice place to stop, where they did a fine plaice and chips (getting silly now, sorry) but the nearby church at St Anthony is steeped in tradition and a superb building. Bish pictured me on its 'chunky pulpit' addressing a non-existent congregation, but nevertheless gave me tips on how to improve my presentation skills.

It was a relatively easy walk along low cliff tops to Portscatho, and its car park. Like I do I engaged in conversation with the Car Park Attendant, with his peaked hat and Man Bag for the tickets and money. I indicated that I was grateful we didn't have to pay him as we were, in fact, car-less which seemed to confuse the poor chap, as then his wife arrived and they got into their car and drove off, seemingly to continue their holiday without harassment. Immediately, however, there on the ground near the entrance was a pig, lying motionless and seemingly ready for the abattoir. In reality said pig was, however, only about an inch long, made of high quality pink Cornish plastic, and soon to accept being called Pasty, and readily took on the role of being our mascot for the rest of the walk.

This was one of our days that simply got better, initially along low cliffs, but they increased in height as we got near Nare Head with its uninterrupted stunning coastal views. Then, as rarely happens but it does occasionally, there on our left, and bang on the path was our overnight accommodation, the Broom Parc Guest House. Probably the poshest place we had stayed in to date, our host Lindsay was brilliant, as was our room with a view over the sea to die for. Known simply as the Red Room, it was tastefully decorated in various shades of blue, and it was sheer pleasure to sit on the loo and look out of the window and enjoy the fantastic uninterrupted views over the English Channel. The breakfast was superb, complete with Marmite for my toast, and I was able to thank Lindsay's Husband, Keith, accordingly. I also shared with him the challenges they faced looking after this fine Georgian property with its 2½ acres, coincidentally owned by the National Trust.

Based on a novel by Mary Wesley called Camomile Lawn, the house was used for a Channel 4 Series released in 1992, and starred Felicity Kendal and Paul Eddington. In case you are wondering, a camomile is a white and yellow daisy like flower.

Day 34. Another healthy 15 mile stretch beckoned, from the brilliant fishing village of Portloe (as also featured in aforementioned series) to the very average setting of Pentewan, and its seemingly enormous Holiday Park. Easily qualifying in the strenuous category, with over 3,000ft of ascent, and as is reliably expected the same magnitude in descent, we were back on the high cliffs, but rich in more of the lush vegetation we had experienced the day before. The great landmark of Dodman (derivation from 'Deadman') Point seemed to haunt us all morning, after reaching it was certainly worth it, being the highest point in south Cornwall, with views back to the Lizard and over to the south Devon coast.

It was getting to the end of the day, raining, as we walked into that well known resort of Mevagissey, which for all intent and purposes, was shut. As we briefly sheltered outside a shop, strangely there was a pop group beating their music out of a covered trailer next to a Bank (remember those buildings?) with the grand audience of two bored groupies. Along the way we passed The Ship Inn (5) reputedly the most flooded pub in the country, and by the end of the year the Landlord reported it had been flooded 12 times in 12 months. He had enough, and soon left, having 'jumped ship'. With no reason to linger we were soon away, with my moment of destiny imminent.

We were guided away from the coast and into some fields, and as we separately looked for a gate or stile to exit, I was immediately charged upon by a rampant herd of cows, maybe, although I wasn't for counting, at least 30 in number. I was soon hemmed in against a six foot high hedge, with no escape.

To say I was scared shitless, is perhaps, an understatement. Not only were the hairs on the back of my neck standing up, and I was sweating profusely, an incident came into my mind a few years earlier when a lady was walking her dogs on the Pennine Way near Hawes, when she was attacked by a herd of cows and killed. It is believed that she may have been trying to protect her dogs, which the cows particularly did not like as they had young calves in the herd. Whilst I only had Pasty to guard, I had no exit strategy as such, and as I could see Bish's ashen face on the top of the hill, not surprisingly, he didn't seem to have one either.

Enter the faithful stick. Since I became a walker I have always used a walking stick, and how folk manage without one, especially on the more rugged ups and downs, I do not know. They are only a bit of a nuisance along the flat, but in this instance it was a Godsend. Not wishing to bring violence into the equation, as there were certainly more of them than me, I started to gently waft my stick in front of their noses and uttered a gentle hissing type noise. Amazingly, after a few minutes, they gradually withdrew and I was able to make my way uninterrupted, and soon, an apparently equally relieved Bish joined me, and gave me an amazing cuddle. We both agreed to keep off milk from then on.

With thankfully no more issues we soon hit Pentewan, and another day ticked off. 363 miles 'safely' negotiated.

Day 35. Just a half day as we were heading home, to Charlestown, 6 miles away. On reflection I may have been a little harsh on my opinion of Pentewan in view of the enormous Holiday Park that dominates the beach and surrounding area, but the town itself is quite quaint and in many ways reminded me of the many fine locations, (such as Grassington) that you find in my beloved Yorkshire Dales. It boasts the fine Ship Inn (6).

But there was no holiday jaunt to follow, and mentally I wasn't tuned in to managing the wild high cliffs, the ups and downs of the rocky coves, and, unusually paths with fences on either side, clearly for preservation purposes. It was soon, however, to be Wordsworth time:

I wandered lonely as a Cloud
That floats on high o'er vales and Hills,
When all at once I saw a crowd
A host of naked wooden ladies;
Besides the Sea, beneath the trees,
Fluttering and dancing in the breeze.

I have the picture to prove it in case you may think I had had too much red wine the night before to celebrate my escape, but even the power of t'internet makes no reference to the purpose of these superbly carved statues, which included an angel and a lion. Maybe they are long gone now, and certainly one of the ladies looked like she was suffering from a bad dose of anorexia. Could have been woodworm, come to think of it.

We battled on, and eventually reached Gerrans Point, with its superb view over St Austell Bay and beyond. And there, looking a bit wind worn was a plaque in memory of A L Rowse, a poet and historian…. "bit like you Vic", Bish exhorted. My book of poems is out there on Amazon should you be the least bit interested.

In his own admission Rowse was a strange individual, and classically was proud to say he didn't speak to ordinary people, unless it was about the weather.

The last sentence on said plaque I just love. It simply reads:

'This was the land of my content.'

Couldn't have said it better, and with some relief we were soon enjoying the beautiful sight of Charlestown, its fascinating Georgian harbour, with its tall ships in dry dock, ready for more Poldark filming.

No time to linger, we would be back there in a year's time. I had a plane to catch.

CHAPTER 12

2013
Charlestown to Wembury

ONLY 262 MILES TO GO, with end point this year of Wembury, some 6 miles to the west of Plymouth, it being 'goodbye to Cornwall' after all these years.

In this year Croatia joined the EU. A magnificent country for a holiday, believe me. Andy Murray won Sports 'Personality' of the Year. In October a report was released that warned of a worldwide wine shortage as demand was outstripping supply. Naturally I stocked up accordingly.

There were some notable deaths, including Nelson Mandela and the one and only Margaret Thatcher. In some places there were street parties celebrating her passing away. We also lost Lou Read, who wrote and sang that great song 'Take a Walk on the Wild side' the lyrics of which were interesting to say the least, and were all about things like transsexuality, drugs, male prostitution and sexual acts. The aforementioned Iron Lady would have put him on the straight and narrow, or have him beheaded, no problem.

Day 36. Back in Charlestown, it was a 10 mile stretch, in theory, to Fowey. A pretty dull day got duller, and the four miles to Par undoubtedly the grottiest stretch of the whole walk. To say the massive holiday complex at Carlyon is ugly is probably not being kind to the folk who actually stay there, and by choice, but is nothing like the china clay works at Spit Point. Fair enough, there has to be the odd industrial zone on the Path, and with steaming chimney tops, settling tanks, dockyards, railways, dumper trucks and giant sheds this certainly put to question my 300 mile drive down south to be there. And we hadn't reached Par itself yet, where even the Ship Inn (7) looked awful. Not even below par, for the golfers out there, a double bogey would have been a fairer score.

To make matters worse, there had been a cliff fall just after Par which meant a 2 miles diversion, with the diversion signs being as clear as the dust that hovered over the whole area; we ended up in a field with the only exit seemingly a 3 foot high barbed wire fence. How we got to Polkeriss please ask Bish, and seeing a pub there he put his hand on my shoulder and said "Vic, I think you need a drink". Even the pint of Doom Bar disappointed.

It had taken us 3 hours to do 5 miles, and I couldn't settle until we reached Gribbin Head, which I knew was a turning point, and there was an 84 ft. red and white hooped tower, effectively a daylight lighthouse, if there is such a thing. It was, however, like the lights had been turned on as we progressed north eastwards, the sun came out, the views to the east were superb, and our destination for the day was in sight.

Before that we dropped down to the beach at Readymoney, which seemed more of a name that could be used for a PayDay Loans operation, but more significantly the place where Dawn French has her modest 40 roomed mansion overlooking the small bay. More about her later, and in no time at all we were in Fowey (pronounced 'Foy') and our pleasant hosts, upon questioning, recommended a nice restaurant for our evening meal where, yes you've got it, Dawn French often dined.

Day 37. It can become a little tiresome for the reader in me raving about the places on this south coast of Cornwall, all with a history, usually a harbour, narrow streets, smashing pubs, including the Ship Inn (8) great pasty shops etc. and Fowey was no exception other than it had more of the type of shops I welcome i.e. not like those selling Cornish ware made in China.

Another great day beckoned, especially having met Dawn French in the pasty shop, she agreed to join us, having read about our exploits in a local Parish Magazine. And what a responsibility too for the Bishop of Sherborne to be accompanied by another vicar, this time the one and only Vicar of Dibley herself.

Defined as a 'strenuous' 12 miles stretch to Looe, reportedly one of the best walking experiences in the whole of the SWCP, there were so many shades of City Blue to admire, from a perfect cloudless sky, peaceful ocean and Dawn's blue trainers, the disappointments of the previous day were soon forgotten as she related many hilarious stories about the filming of the series and the characters involved.

For most part of this morning it was cliff walking in its purest form, no roads or car parks, and only one isolated house, once employed as a lookout near Dodman Point. At Lansallos Cove, a picture postcard setting if there ever was one, and not a single soul in sight, Dawn got a call from her agent and said she had to return home immediately. I got her to sign the dvd box set of the Vicar of Dibley Series I had in my rucksack, and for the first time in my life I was kissed by a Vicar; The Bishop shook her hand, and in no time at all, she was gone.

And if you believe the last few paragraphs I will have a little laugh at your expense, sorry, but I did have fun writing them. Joking apart, and I have seen her in the flesh at Southport Theatre in her 'One Woman Show', she is a tremendous individual who I admire greatly. I just love people who don't take themselves seriously.

More remoteness and natural beauty followed, and having passed through a small wooded area, there was Polperro, and another of those moments in time us walkers dream of. Literally on the path, one step to my left would take me into The Blue Peter Inn (as favoured by Christopher Trace and Valerie Singleton) whilst one step to the right, as preferred by Bish would take him into the village itself. No decision here for me to take, we agreed to meet up in an hour's time.

As I ordered my pint of Tribute at the bar, I couldn't help but notice the northern voice besides me, from a lady who distinctly sounded like she was from my neck of the woods. As is my usual wont, I took the bullock by the horns and said to her "You sound like a true Bolton lass to me". To which she replied: "I am, I'm from Horwich…how did you know that?"

There followed about an hour and a half of conversation with her and her husband, a great couple, and it soon transpired that she did, in fact, work for Bolton Council who also employed me from 1998 to 2007. She admitted she couldn't recall me (not surprisingly as she worked in the Commissioning Division, Eastern Ward, Section 2) but seemed to recognise my name and had seen me pictured in the Bolton News. And after exchanging drinks, like you do, and three pints later, I staggered out into the bright sunshine to look for my friend, who was sat by the harbour having a fag, checking his phone, and feeding the gulls. As if….

There is more to Polperro than the bar at the Blue Peter Inn, and so special it has to be a place, sorry to say this, to avoid in the height of the summer should you wish not to be trampled on by fellow tourists munching on pilchard sandwiches. We still had five tough miles before we got to Looe.

I am reminded of a great book by Shally Hunt, who in 1995, with her husband, also it is believed to be of sound body and mind, decided to walk the whole way round England and Scotland, a mere 4250 miles. Starting in Eastbourne they walked westwards towards Land's End and continued their clockwise adventure accordingly. It only took them 10 months, and her book is titled 'The sea on our Left'.

When you have had 3 pints of strong local ale, it has to be irresponsible to walk along a coastal path in south Cornwall, with the sea to your **right,** especially when your only functioning eye is definitely on the left side of your face. Thankfully Bish has two good eyes, and the path was generally wide enough for him to keep an eye on me (pun intended). I am assured the scenery was equally as appealing as before 'lunch', and a bit like rushing to the toilet, we were soon at the lavatorial place of Looe, and our day's destination.

I remember going to a friend's house in my teens, and I couldn't believe they had two loos, one downstairs (albeit purple coloured) and one upstairs. I thought they were dead rich and couldn't wait to get home and tell my parents.

There are, in fact, two Looes, one in the east which we passed through, and one in the west amazingly titled West Looe, where our Guest House was situated overlooking the estuary. Our kindly host, who incidentally I never warmed to, immediately indicated that we had been upgraded (always nice to hear) adding thereafter that they had no other guests staying that night. And no, I will not make any jokes about there being a loo in the room.

Not sure about Looe despite its rave reviews, or where we ate that night, but it had been another fine day to remember, and before we knew it, another Dawn was breaking and we were soon on our way again.

Day 38. This 17 mile day was to see us walk to the charming village of Kingsand, via a superbly named place called Portwrinkle.

In leaving Looe we passed by the Ship Inn (9) and I guess

by now you are getting the hang of the numbering system I have adopted. I missed the one in Polperro for obvious reasons, and I am sure the local CAMRA representative will tell me about others en route I simply overlooked, but I remain more than intrigued that there is a Ship Inn in Leeds City Centre, and would you believe in my beloved St Helens...complete, if you visit the website, with the proud boast that they have a plasma screen outside.

After such an invigorating previous day, this day was largely a bit of an anti-climax, but a time for reflection can never do any harm, with still the odd moment to savour.

'Moderate' walking saw us pass by the very average village of Seaton, and soon followed by us missing the very Irish sounding Downderry, which the route planner seemed to want us not to see before reaching Portwrinkle. As I say, great name, but as a location just a few houses, a car park and not a Ship Inn in sight. From there we passed our first golf course (why spoil a good walk?) and into a firing range, but this of the gun variety, being part of the Tregantle Fort complex, completed in 1865, built to deter the French from attacking the naval bases along this southern coast. With no red flags flying this was an interesting section, if not slightly intimidating. Long Sands below was a four mile long beach, above which seemed a mass of unloved wooden chalets of various shapes and sizes. We soon were to get our first glimpse of Plymouth, but then no civilisation round Rame Head, known locally as Cornwall's Forgotten Garden, before walking north east towards Cawsand, immediately linked with Kingsand, and with their stone coloured washed stone cottages, probably our last view of yet another delightful setting in this wonderful county. The Cliff House didn't disappoint in any shape or form, the morning's breakfast up there with the very best to date.

The local pub served us well, and it was time for reflection as tomorrow we would be leaving Cornwall, and back into Devon. I guess to say that you have walked all the way round Cornwall would look good on your CV, being a total of 290 miles, give or take the odd diversion. It certainly had its contrasts, with the exposed north Cornish coast, with very few harbours and the long Atlantic rollers loved by the surfers, being in many ways much bleaker than the more picturesque south coast characterised by delightful little villages and coves. My favourite spot remains as Porthleven although Polperro runs it a close second. The Bishop favoured St Ives, but like me the view from Hawker's Hut, the day we saw it, remains high up in the memory stakes. South Devon certainly had a lot to live up to.

Day 39. Final day of this year was to see us get to Wembury about 12 miles away, depending how you gauge our efforts to negotiate Plymouth, the only city we had to walk through on the Path. The ferry from Cremyll took us into the large harbour area. Steeped in history, and heavily bombed in the Second World War, I was quite looking forward to something totally different to what we had experienced to date, especially as, this being a Sunday, things should be reasonably quiet. Then, as we got off the ferry boat, it seemed like one enormous human cyclone had hit us straight in the face.

After the peacefulness and solitude we had enjoyed since Looe, we were in a people hell. They were everywhere, on the pavements, on the roads and some hanging out of windows shouting their heads off. There were officials everywhere, all seemingly dressed in some form of yellow, some of the First Aid variety, some Traffic Wardens and some definitely looking like the Police. There was music blaring out, and drink stations everywhere. Then there was this old man in shorts staggering in the middle of the road towards us, looking like he had seen 70 many years ago, with people cheering him to keep going towards all the activity on the hill to his right.

We had walked straight into the end part of Plymouth's Annual Half Marathon, a major event in the City's calendar. No sightseeing for us, as all I wanted to do was to locate the ferry to Mount Batten Point, our escape to normality, and back onto the Path. And as we got to the boat, there was a long queue full of weary runners, medals round their neck clutching their goody bags, friends, and parents with small people who had also run, dogs, seagulls, oh I could go on. Luckily we got on the ferry as I looked longingly into Plymouth's impressive harbour and land to the east side which would return us to where we belonged. Bish bemoaned the fact we hadn't gone to the Mayflower Steps. "Is that a pub?" I retorted.

There is little to be written about the rest of the day as we reached our destination at the estuary of the River Yealm in good time, and we had to walk a few miles back to our cars at Langdon Court. Our return to Devon had not made a good start, although with 426 miles now under our belt, only 200 miles or so now to go.

Later in the year I was fortunate enough to go to Canada. The story of my time there is contained with my other stories later in this book. And for the record, it has the longest coastline in the world. At only 125,567 miles in length, a walk along it would be some challenge!

CHAPTER 13

2014
Wembury to Torcross

A MEMORABLE YEAR, in more ways than one, in what was the country's warmest year since records began, at average temperature of almost 10 degrees centigrade. Certainly, after an overcast start this May, the days just got better as we headed towards our end destination of Torcross.

In this year the South Devon railway wall near Dawlish was washed away in a torrential storm, and the pressure was on to get it repaired before Bish&Vic passed through the following year. Kate Bush became the first female artist to have eight albums in the UK Album charts, and I can't name one of them. We lost Tom Finney, Rik Mayall, Richard Attenborough and the MH370 on its way from Kuala Lumpur to Beijing. I still can't get my head round that one, nor why, in this year, Facebook paid US$19bn for What's App.

One of many challenges facing a long distance walker is what to carry in the rucksack, bearing in mind it is nice to have something fresh and clean to change into in the evening after a long days trek. After 12 years on this walk, and having undertaken previous long trails, I believe I had got it right in that I never had a particularly large bag, chose lightweight clothes being a believer in the 'layers' principle, and kept toiletries to the bare minimum, choosing for example those brush and tooth paste sets they give you in some hotels, and a single Bic razor. And thank you for Crocs, which only came into being the year before we started the walk. Originally developed as a nursing shoe, they feel so good after a long day in heavy boots.

'Two old crocs on the South West Coastal Path'. Sounds like a good title for a book, methinks.

And, as you are probably already aware, I always have a stick, originally of the wooden variety now more of metal/plastic constructions known as poles, and I often see walkers with two of them. I tried that once, one was called Wojciech and the other had an equally unpronounceable name. Sorry I knew I would get some stick for that one.

But this year saw a change on this front, and the introduction of a new challenge, which, for want of a better expression is called 'Car Hopping'. Bish, a keen and very good badminton player, was taking part in a Bishops v Bankers Match in Banbury, when he hurt his back going for a difficult shot. He denies he made a cock-up of it, but it certainly harmed his back to the extent that carrying anything of weight on it thereafter put him in great pain. He had even walked on the Dorset Downs with some old bibles in his rucksack to see if he could manage, but alas, to no avail.

The consequences therefore meant that the days of us carrying all our gear on our backs for the duration of the year's walk were no longer, and each day we had to ensure our non-walking gear, and a car, was at the end of it.

Day 40. I arranged for us to meet at the All Saints church in Holbeton, so that we could have a quick word with the Big Boss before setting off again on our adventures. Then, looking for Bish on the road overlooking the village I saw a flash of yellow like something I had never seen before in my life. It was like the sun was exploding, it had become rectangular and it was rapidly heading towards me down the hill. It then became clear that this was, in fact the Bishop, in a brilliant yellow Datsun Nissan, with a personalised number plate thrown in. He advised that this was his daughter's car he had borrowed, in order to bring a bit of sunshine into the proceedings. It didn't seem possible that the same little girl I had seen in Minehead back in 2003, who was at primary school then, now had her own car. And there was me, still in the same waterproof I was wearing all those years ago.

Explanations and statutory greetings exchanged, Bish's face suddenly became vexed as he saw my stick, and whilst he doesn't swear, only over the good book of course, he then realised he had left **his** behind in **his** car. I will stick with this story, but return to it later.

This was to be a relatively straightforward 7 miles stretch from Noss Mayo (with Ship Inn No.10) to the picturesque Erme Estuary, which has often been described as England's most unspoiled estuary. Also a pretty dangerous one too for walkers, as it is possible to 'wade' across it either side of low water along an old ford, and under normal conditions it is about knee deep, with a river bed of sinking sand and pebbles. Super eh? But in our case, enter car hopping, as we were to start the following day on the other side.

It was tough going from Noss Mayo, initially through some woods, which you know I love, but on this occasion the grassland was covered in blue bells, and a stunning sight. The weather was bordering on the miserable, and with absolutely nothing along the route, other than ups and downs, some perilously near the edge, Bish was soon bemoaning that this was a stick-less day to get through as quickly as possible. Which we successfully did.

Every cloud invariably has a silver lining, and our evening was spent at the superb Dolphin Inn in nearby Kingston. A lovely village, the pub is on one side of a narrow alley way (the

Cumbrians would call it a ginnel) and accommodation on the other. There is a sign which says 'Please drive quietly through our pub'.

I got to know the landlord, Geoff, quite well, and learnt that he had been a Solicitor for 35 years, originally from Oldham, but finishing up in Plymouth, and having initially had a small B&B, loved it so much he bought the Dolphin in 2002, and was in fact only its 5th landlord since the war. Having spent the bulk of his life advising on divorce, he loved the life he had there. On enquiry I asked him what his secret was to running such a successful enterprise, and his reply was simple: "I wake up every morning smiling". To top it all, he was also a keen walker, and willingly lent Bish his stick who, would you believe, woke up the next day.... 'Smiling!!'.

Day 41. Only 8 miles this day, generally of the easy but occasionally strenuous variety, would see us end up at Inner Hope, but we probably drove at least 40 miles in the process. We were very much in the South Hams farmlands, characterised not only by its estuaries but more significantly, by its narrow country lanes. These generally ran from north to south, and not surprisingly the Path ran from west to east.

It took me back to my childhood, in my Dad's old Ford, and nothing seemed to have changed, except I was driving this time. Signposts were non-existent or horizontal to the ground. The lanes were invariably single track, with numerous impossible blind corners, and naturally, as some of you will know, had grass growing in the middle. You dreaded meeting anyone coming the other way as there were no passing places and the hedgerows to the side always seemingly at least ten foot high.

Now I rarely argue with the fairer sex, on the basis that I never win, but on this particularly day I felt like throwing this particularly well spoken, authoritative and stingingly boring lady in my car off the highest cliff and into the raging English

Channel below. Whilst looking for our various start points she would tell me to do U turns in these impossible narrow lanes, tell me turn left into what was obviously a farm yard, sometimes saying nothing at all, and then at the top of the Avon Estuary had me heading back to Plymouth when clearly I needed to be travelling in the other direction. In the end I switched her off and threw her onto the back seat and relied on what I should have used in the first place...a map, a compass and a bit of good old common sense.

The Bish had similar problems with the SatNavLady in his bananamobile, as being Japanese he couldn't understand a word she was saying, being more interested in directing him to the nearest YO! Sushi, of which you will appreciate there are not many in South Devon.

Lest we forget, I know I should be telling you about the walking, which up to Bigbury-on-Sea was stunning, with some seriously high cliff faces and interesting climbs and ascents. Indeed it was great not to have a load on my back, but not so great was the descent down to Challaborough and its immense caravan park. Certainly more pleasing was the gentle stroll into Bigbury-on-Sea itself, complete with Burgh Island opposite, which you can walk to when the tide is out. Dominated by its Art Deco Hotel, built in the 1930's, I think it spoilt the overall visage, but it maybe is one of those places that look better from the inside looking out.

It was an uncomplicated and gentle stroll to our evening stop at Inner Hope, having passed through Outer Hope, a very pleasant area. For reasons long lost in the memory I had booked us single rooms, and naturally, being the Leader of the Pack, there was No Hope for Bish that I would not be in the bigger and better of the two.

As I dozed off to sleep that night, thinking of things like you do on such occasions, I thought about the day, which in truth is best described as navigational, and the high and low points. No problem with the latter, it being **that** woman, in **my** car, telling **me** where to go. The highlight had to be the Bish kindly letting me drive, for the first time, a brand new, sparkling, stunningly yellow top of the range Datsun, which in itself, would bring sunshine into anyone's life. I was only allowed to drive it round the car park though.

Day 42. We were certainly not making much impact on the milometer this year, as today was certainly a short one, with an easy car hop to Salcombe, and if it was 5 miles walking I would be exaggerating. This was purposeful, however, as there was nowhere to stay for a considerable distance after the town, and anyway I had heard and read that it was a special place, and my mate Geoff told me about the Ferry Inn, which as you would guess, was not hard to locate.

There is precious little to say about the day's walk other than it was stunningly special, not only in its scenery and remoteness, but there was to be no route march. We could genuinely take in the beauty of it all, the spectacular high cliffs, the inaccessible coves below, and despite this being a Saturday, not a soul in sight. Amazingly almost, this being a coastal walk, we almost took a wrong turning! The view from Bolt Tail gave us great views back over Bigbury Bay and beyond, whilst after about 4 miles ambling gently along, we reached Bolt Head, at the head of the estuary on which Salcombe happily sits. This was a special setting which I will always treasure, photographs taken and shared, and a gentle stroll followed into what was, in truth, another world.

The Ferry Inn didn't disappoint, it having great views, as you would expect, of the ferry that crossed the Kingsbury Estuary. We were able to sit outside, take it all in, as what seemed like hundreds of tourist- like persons passed by. In fact, it has been reported that the population of Salcombe is about two thousand, but it increases to about twenty thousand at the height of the summer season.

A yachting centre of great self-esteem, there is an air of prosperity about the place, and it has been known to be called the 'Kensington-on-Sea'. We were clearly underdressed to walk its streets, or to be exact its main street known as Fore Street, deemed to be, by the Daily Telegraph, the sixth 'coolest' street in the country. All the shops were distinctly up market, having names I had never heard of, many selling clothes with brands, I am led to believe, of the highest order. We took refuge in a café, which used to be a branch of the Midland Bank. We sat near the safe door, and like you do, reminisced. We paid for our tea and black forest gateau out of our pension monies which the Bank kindly bestowed upon us, for long service to the cause.

You can't drive or park in Salcombe, the main car park being about a mile up the hill, and another half mile to our B&B for the night. En route we passed by a local Estate Agents. It is reputed to be as expensive to buy a posh house here as it is in Sandbanks, and a view in the shop window indicated that you didn't get much for your million pounds, and certainly not a view over the estuary. For a sea view you had to be as rich as good old Harry Redknapp.

Day 43. Sunday 11 May was to be the day of an ecstatic Frenchman, a delirious Belgian, a mad Englishman and a bemused Curate amongst others. First we had to get to Torcross, some 14 miles away, defined as 'strenuous', and some 467 miles into the Path. A special day to be treasured, and one of those days that just simply got better and better.

After getting one car to our destination it was back to the car park in Salcombe, down into the town, a visit to the Pasty shop (of course), and ferry across to East Portlemouth, a walk south of the village and we were away, and away far from the madding crowds. Then the Bishop exclaimed "I haven't got my stick" or to be more exact, he hadn't got Geoff's stick. After a brief discussion that took all of 10 seconds, we had no alternative but to turn back. Admittedly, to lose something you own is not good news, but to lose something that is not yours in the first place, is a double whammy. The problem we faced that day was that Bish couldn't remember when he last had it. And neither could I, come to think of it.

Silence reigned as we re-ferried back to Salcombe, and whilst Bish retraced his steps, I worked on Plan B in trying to find somewhere where we might be able to buy a replacement. I walked past shops with names such as Weird Fish, Sea Chest, Joules, Sea Salt, Deck Out all of which must mean something to some of you out there, and thought my luck may be in as I found one called Bob and Fred, which possibly sold men's gear, or could even help me in my quest. The shop assistant immediately looked me up and down as if I had just disembarked from some alien craft that had docked in the harbour, and upon enquiry responded that they didn't sell that sort of item in her shop. When I asked if there was any shop in Salcombe that sold walking sticks, she emphatically replied "Not that I know of......you may wish to try establishments in Plymouth".

Suitably dismissed, who should be walking down the street, waving at me with something that remarkably looked like Geoff's pole in his hand, was a smiling Bish. Some kind lady in the Pasty Shop had rescued it for him. Back to the ferry, where I gave him some stick, like he would have done in return no doubt, as we walked up the other side of the estuary overlooking the town I thought, like the opposite to the view I had had of the hotel on Burgh Island, that Salcombe was better to look at than actually to visit, from my perspective anyway. And with a blink of an eye, it was gone and a serious days walking lay ahead.

The sea and sky were brilliant shades of contrasting pure blue, and our next goal was Prawle Point, the most southern point in Devon, and we were to walk northwards now for a year or so. After some easy walking across some fields, what should we find, but Kate Bush's house, or one of them at least. Hence my reference to her earlier, the artiste of Wuthering Heights fame, and this property is called Lingering Lows (as if!). Renowned for her almost obsessive desire for privacy, why should she choose a property on a coastal path as popular as this one I wondered? There has been a lot of controversy about its security systems, access roads, plans to divert footpaths etc. as the arguments continue to this day. There must be a song title in it somewhere...will have to think about that one.

After walking over the superb looking Lannacombe Beach, we were warned to keep well away from the cliff edge, being grateful again for our faithful sticks and soon we were approaching Start Point, another iconic setting with lighthouse thrown in. Looking truly north now, the view took us to our day's destination on Start Bay and ironically had a signpost which indicated Poole was a mere 168 miles away.

After a steep descent it was all very gentle now, and into Beesands, in which Bish was amazed that I walked straight past its pub, the famous Cricket Inn, which had survived storms, a World War II bomb and a mudslide. I had my eye firmly set on a nearby local play area, complete with full size football pitch where I sat, on what was clearly the coach's bench. It was 4.54pm, and I switched on my phone, took a deep breath, looked up to perfect blue sky above, looked down and the message from Elaine read "We did it!! 2-0. Nasri and Kompany. Champions again!" These gentlemen are, in case you didn't know, from France and Belgium respectively.

I went a bit berserk. Bish later describes seeing a hitherto sensible former banker charge off, arms aloft, onto the football pitch, cheering loudly something about a blue moon, romp round the centre circle, ripping off his top in sheer delight, and returning to him and planting a huge kiss on his forehead.

Being a Yeovil fan himself he couldn't see what all the fuss was about, whilst my boots didn't touch the ground on our final mile into Torcross. There we had a celebratory pint, and went looking for a tank, like you do.

Last car hop of the year saw me back in Torcross for a night alone in the posh Linger Lodge, with Elaine joining me the night following. I went back to the pub, dined and drank alone, pondered about a very special day in my life, and, believe it or not, felt quite miserable, because, as I may have said before, 'What is happiness if you can't share it?' Whilst this was undoubtedly a wonderful part of the country and I had had a great day, I could bet that being in Manchester that night would have been a pretty exciting experience.

As luck would have it, I found out later that the chap who

took my place in the Bank when I left in 1997, lived in a nearby town called Kingsbridge, and we could have met up that night. He's got a lovely wife too.

As for the Kate Bush song, guess it has to be 'Running up that Hill'.

CHAPTER 14

2015 (Part 1)
Torcross to Dawlish Warren

M Y PLANNING FOR THIS year was largely dictated by
the need to get to Starcross, a distance of some 48,
(certainly varied) miles. This would mean that we started next
time the other side of the River Exe. We sort of achieved this
goal, although the purists may differ, more of which later.

It was May time, still my favourite month for walking,
again no waterproofs required, sunshine and freshness
everywhere, and driving down, played one of my favourite
Runrig tracks, with lyrics:

I'm alive again on a May morning
Going to wipe the slate clean
Follow my dreams
All the young buds are born again
With the promise of a new life to come
Spring is here again.

The sun is melting over the hills
All the roads are waiting
To be revealed
For this day in history had brought us to here

Now it's all there for the taking
The day is what you see.

The light's returning, the work is to hand
All the cynics have vanished
From where we stand
All the chances wasted are drawing me near
And all around there's new life rising
From the winter fields.

Called May Morning, look it up on YouTube, especially the live versions. You won't be disappointed.

The logistics for this year worked out to plan, although a new world opened out for me which I personally found interesting, enlightening and certainly, in some quarters, highly amusing.

Day 44. It was about 10 miles from Torcross to Dartmouth, both iconic places in their own right, but first we had to get back to Torcross. I had cunningly booked us into Chris and Carol's fine Guest House in Brixham for two nights. Eat your heart out Mr Misery Guts! Carol, also more formally known as Mrs Robinson, brought back memories of what was, and maybe still is, one of my favourite films, The Graduate, and the music of Simon and Garfunkel.

From Brixham I was back in the Bish's Yellow Peril to Kingswear where we left it, crossed the ferry to Dartmouth, and then got the bus down to Torcross.....on a double decker bus. I think I may have been at school when I last was on one, and this being Thursday 7 May a more momentous event than  the General Election that also happened to be on this day, as I was to use my Old Gits Bus Pass for the very first time. Bish kindly showed me how to use it, and said we could sit upstairs at the front. As it was such a special event, he took a great picture by way of celebration, and the views along Start Bay I enjoyed for the cost of absolutely nothing.

When we arrived at Torcross I congratulated the driver for undertaking an immaculate three point turn in Slapton along the route then he asked where we were walking to. "Dartmouth", I replied. He didn't respond.

Torcross is a fabulous setting, with the sands and sea on one side, and a fresh water lake to its west, Slapton Ley, which was formed in the Ice Age. It is a national nature reserve amongst other things and is renowned for its ecology and wildlife. The area itself, however, was incredibly home to one of the most tragic events of the whole Second World War.

It was evacuated in 1943, like many other villages in the area, to accommodate thousands of allied troops, mainly Americans. Slapton Sands were very similar to the beaches seen in Normandy, and it was used for a dress rehearsal for the D-Day landings in the spring of 1944. On 28 April 1944, an incredible 30,000 American troops were loaded on to landing craft and taken out into the bay to practice coming ashore. By sheer chance there were nine German torpedo boats in the area that saw what was going on and were able to blow some of the landing craft out of the water.

How many troops died that day is uncertain. A commemorative plaque indicates 749 Americans were killed, although the actual figure is probably more like 1,000. For morale purposes, and to keep the planning process secret, it was all kept very quiet, although certainly more were killed then, than in the actual landings themselves a month later. There is also a Sherman amphibious tank in the village, which was salvaged from the shallow waters of the bay in 1984, as a result of the sterling efforts of a local hotelier, Ken Small.

Over the years Torcross has survived battering from some

terrible storms, especially in 1979 and 2001, but more recently in February 2014 which caused extensive damage to all the properties along the promenade, they being hit by green water that came over the sea wall, and the road looked like the beach with all the sand and pebbles that came with it.

How peaceful it all seemed this brilliantly sunny day in May, as, for the first time in forty odd days of walking, it was in a straight line for a few miles, before we headed inland, and we didn't see a lot of the coast until, after another golden mile, we reached Blackpool; and we hadn't even seen the famous tower first either. More correctly known as Blackpool Sands, it looked a great setting, but being privately owned, and us poor pensioners, we were certainly not for paying to get in. Dogs are banned too. After a few ups and downs, a short trip around Dartmouth Castle, we were soon in the town itself, steeped in history and a great setting. Unfortunately (for Bish anyway) we had a ferry to catch, and in no time we were back in Brixham.

Over a pleasant evening meal, I shared with Bish the time, in 1970, I went with my then fiancé, still my present wife, to see the two and only Simon and Garfunkel, at the Royal Albert Hall. Our tickets, which weren't bad, cost fifteen shillings (75p) each, and their signature song of the day, Bridge Over Troubled Water, was still flying high. Garfunkel sang it alone at the front, whilst Simon sat on a table at the back, with a deadpan face. When I later read Simon's autobiography, it was ironic when speaking about their acrimonious split up soon after, that he wrote "at least I got my song back".

In 2004 I was fortunate enough to see them (re-united) again in Manchester. Then both aged 63, it was a brilliant concert. Simon said "We don't argue anymore. We're exhausted". The tickets cost a mere £56 each, and Art still appeared to be wearing the same black waistcoat. To cap it all, as I write this in 2016, Paul Simon can be seen in

Manchester…tickets priced at £100 !!

Day 45. For the second time running, the General Election passed us by, especially as I couldn't get the television in our room to work. For the election 'too close to call' through the power of t'internet we learnt that the Tories were looking at a 30 something majority. All talk later seemed to be how the pollsters had got it so wrong, not how many people were gutted that poor Ed Milliband wasn't going to get to see the Queen for tea that day. I don't really do politics, but can't help feeling that things may have been a lot different if the party had chosen his brother to lead them when they had the chance.

Back to the real world, and this was to be a tough day of some 11 miles and nearly 3,000 feet ascent, from Kingswear back to Brixham. I got to use my bus pass again, and what with getting a lamb tikka pasty and can of Red Bull, the days walking was to cost me all of four pounds. What I hadn't appreciated was that we were to embark on probably the toughest and most remote section of the whole coastal path, and what lay ahead after Brixham in the days following being best described as messy.

Leaving behind the very pleasant Dart Estuary, we soon appreciated a superb spread of bluebells in woods south of Kingswear, and after turning north eastwards at Outer Forward Point we came across the unique terraced gardens of Coleton Fishacre with exotic plants, I am reliably informed, from South America, China and B & Q. Dogs were welcomed too.

When the going gets tough, they say, the tough get going and it was certainly that for the next few miles, and after passing Crabrock Point came another of those moments, which isn't easy to explain, but it did happen M'Lord…..I was photographed by the Bishop kissing a lady's nipple, her left one to be precise. Clearly the highlight of the day by far, the low point has to be was that it belonged to a seriously wooden lady who was looking out to sea with great intent.

Like the previous occasion near Pentewan we did not have a clue what it was doing there, who carved it and why, but it was a magnificent piece of art which would brighten up any clergyman's day.

The going got easier as we reached Shoalstone Point, and we could see Paignton and Torquay ahead in the distance, and it was to be a sad farewell to the peace and tranquillity, undulating landscape, immense cliffs and isolated coves which characterised South Devon.

Brixham is in a fine setting, and was once one of the largest fisheries in the country. We were happy to take stock as we sat on a bench overlooking its harbour, and which contains a full size reconstruction of Drake's Golden Hind. A bit too colourful for my liking, you could pay to go on it, but I had already spent my day's allowance.

Day 46. We were to head for Babbacombe, approximately 13 miles to the north, and which is described in the guide as being an urban section. We were heading for the English Riviera, with the strap line of "a lifetime of memories", full of award winning beaches, exotic palm trees, and voted England's top seaside destination. In case you think I am back on the malt whisky, this is Paignton and Torquay we are talking about.

We got lost trying to get out of Brixham, which you will appreciate is pretty hard to do on a coastal walk, but as ever I could blame it on the woods and the day didn't get any better. All I can remember about Paignton are its beach huts, and Torquay, which had a big wheel, like a mini London Eye. Al Stewart was playing that night at the Theatre House, but I had already seen him in Manchester in April. Tickets were £25 each. But what were all these people doing here, just wandering aimlessly about eating ice creams and going in and out of shops, or just sitting outside cafes with coffee cups with digestives to hand, reading the Daily Mirror, talking about the meaning of life, and other inconsequential things? No sign of Basil Fawlty either.

I then got a call from Elaine. She had locked herself out of the house. Fortunately we had a friend in the village who was good at breaking into houses. Problem soon solved, and we pottered on.

We eventually got through the crowds to Babbacombe, a little more refined location, loved by Queen Victoria who wrote in 1846 "It's a beautiful spot....red cliffs and rocks with wooded hills like Italy". Her full review you can find on TripAdvisor. The highlight of the day, however, was that I was back on a bus again, and back to Torquay, changed to yet another bus that got us back to Brixham, and yes, you've got it, cars back to Babbacombe and our stay at the imaginatively named Babbacombe Palm Guest House.

The front was full of eating houses which didn't appeal, so we ended up at a posh Fish and Chip Shop. The owner was surprised that we hadn't booked, but recognising me as a famous author and walker, found us a table under the stairs by the kitchen. Pleasingly licensed, with a glass of Chilean Merlot to hand, we toasted a great day. I jest, of course, but then shared with Bish my decision to temporarily suspend him as my walking partner, and replace him, by........a dog!! No ordinary one, mind you, a bearded collie with a fine pedigree, her Great Grandmother had won Best of Breed at Crufts of all places/events.

I think he appreciated my rationale, being the gentleman he is. Admittedly he lives in one of our finest counties, and had already walked the Dorset Coast Path, which was soon to follow in our travels. My rationale was that I could share a holiday with Elaine in the county, cover areas he knew well anyway, and introduce Rosie to its beautiful and enchanting countryside. She had also always wanted to go to Dogchester.

Day 47. A difficult long day, which is putting it mildly, saw me planning, as best I could, for us to finish the walk on the western side of the Exe Estuary, nearly 15 miles distant, and with the first half pretty strenuous, with many ups and downs, as we aimed for Shaldon. Easy thereafter, it was journeys end at Starcross (ish).

We were back to car hopping, and had the Teign Estuary to negotiate, and the first half of the day to Teignmouth (pronounced 'Tinmuth') was memorable for being unmemorable, quiet and not many views to recall. The town itself, once a busy port and shipbuilding centre, is now a pleasant resort, renowned in days gone by for segregating male and female bathers on either side of the pier. All I recall is its car park, and then a long walk along its sea wall before we started our love affair with the A379 and Brunel's railway. It is amazing how the line clings faithfully to the coast, and the collapsed area in Dawlish was repaired to our entire satisfaction.

I was last in Dawlish on Friday 11 August 1972 to be exact. Things in life, I am told are either meant to be ('fate' I think they call it) or just happen by chance. I had married my childhood sweetheart six days earlier, and neither of us still can't believe why on earth we chose to go to Dawlish for our honeymoon, and on that day we were to drive some 200 miles into deepest Kent for another wedding. We were in an old Austin A30 with only one windscreen wiper working, and the following Monday 14th August I was to start work at F W Woolworth & Co. in sunny Bolton. Bizarrely, for eight months of my life, I was able to walk to work too!

We had little money at the time, and pre t'internet it wasn't as easy to gauge your accommodation, and we had chosen a very average family run 'hotel' on the outskirts of the town which was overrun by families with ill-disciplined children, and the new Mrs Bullock, having been a teacher then for a year, knew one of them when she saw one. Other than going to Plymouth one day I can't recall much about our time in Dawlish. Guess we must have just stayed in bed.

With no memories to share, Dawlish passed me by again as we headed along the railway line and alongside some very impressive red cliffs to Dawlish Warren, colonised by caravan parks and entertainment arcades, but thankfully on to its famous nature reserve, renowned for all sorts of plants and birds never seen anywhere else in the country. We went as far as we could towards its point on the peninsula, working out that walking back an equal distance we had covered what would have been the equivalent mileage to Starcross, a place we were never to see, but apparently we didn't miss much anyway.

Driving back to Tinmuth the Bish, following on to the previous night's conversation, said: "So you are replacing me, as your walking partner, with a dog". I thought carefully about giving a response that would not offend, and trying once in my life to be caring and sensitive, but all I could come up with was…. "Yes, I suppose I am…"

CHAPTER 15

2015 (Part 2)
Lyme Regis to Kimmeridge Bay

W E HAD REACHED THE business end of the walk, with a mere 115 miles to go. Up to now I had been boringly logistical in starting the year where we had finished the year previous. With the goal of finishing in 2016, calculator out, in each of our 13 years since 2003 we had managed to walk a mind boggling 40 miles a year. Quality rather than quantity, except for the odd blip around Barnstaple and Torquay, I had loved every step of the way. Without using my fingers, that's another 3 years walking to do, and I was getting impatient, especially as I had other long distance walks in mind, many of which I hadn't shared with my wife. That one in Canada certainly looked interesting.

Hence my cunning plan to do as much of the Dorset Coast Path as I could with Rosie, who was barking mad at me to get on with my plan, hence to go down in July of this year, and leave four days in 2016 to reach journey's end and celebrations at South Haven Point in Poole Harbour.

Then the Ministry of Defence, bless them, stepped in as the Army Range between Lulworth and Kimmeridge could only be passed through at weekends. This resulted in us (that is me and Rosie) not being able to do the walk in strict geographical order as hitherto, but eh, whose walk was this anyway and I could still claim my certificate from the SWCP Association.

No car hopping either, as we only had one, that being MB Taxis, nor buses…my pass had expired and non-guide dogs are not allowed on them anyway.

Day 48. All very messy and not easy to plan, as the storms over the winter had meant many landslips in the area, and which meant us starting to the west of Lyme Regis and climbing Golden Cap, ending up at West Bexington some 13 miles away. We were dropped off at the start, whilst Elaine did Lyme Regis, the 'Pearl of Dorset' and other things that ladies do when left to their own devices.

Fortunately it was a fine day, and a surprisingly easy walk to the top of Golden Cap, at 617 feet the highest point on the South Coast. Not that Rosie is not good on the lead, anxious to get to the top she sort of pulled me up, and we had a tremendous view back towards Devon and eastwards, initially to West Bay.

Also at the top, it all changed. People started to smile and talk to me and you know why….I had a dog with me, and a good looking one too. No disrespect, of course, to the Bishop, who is also quite good looking for his advanced years, we are a nation of dog lovers, with, I am led to believe, over 8 million dogs out there……quite a lot to choose from. Indeed, half of their owners seem to walk their dogs with lead in one hand, and mobile phone in the other, you may have noticed.

It was a gentle walk down to Seatown, and the Anchor Inn. There I am sure I saw Julia Bradbury (commonly often referred to as the walking man's crumpet) sitting outside with a pint. Seeing us she jumped up and started to walk towards us. Not to me, I assure you, but to say 'Hello' to Rosie. I then introduced myself as a famous author and walker, as she exclaimed that my book 'Journeys' which you can still buy at Awesome Books for £17.68 plus postage should you not have a copy, had inspired her to do what she was doing with her life. Her Producer then called out for her and she was gone. We can all dream, eh? In truth, the pub was shut and we walked on by.

Memories abound for you Midland Bank Bolton people out there; you may recall the odd walk yourself down Bradshawgate to another Anchor Inn, now unfortunately long closed. Often referred to as my second office, I was supporting a customer, Eric Dew, who served a fine pint of Bass, and his brilliant steak baguettes, which he named 'World Famous', certainly were. I entertained customers there, who also loved it, and we had many a staff leaving do there, often behind closed doors. And on one famous occasion a member of staff, who I shall not name, but he was called Alan, fell asleep in the men's loo (no mobiles then) and was rescued in the early hours of the morning as his pleas for rescue were eventually heard as he poked his head out of the toilet window and yelled for help.

Seatown, which only has the pub and a few thatched cottages, is also famous for the place in Thomas Hardy's superb novel, the Mayor of Casterbridge, where at a country fair, a young hay-trusser Michael Henchard, got so drunk on rum that he decided to auction off his wife and baby daughter, selling them to a sailor for five guineas. No eBay then, he swore never to touch drink again, and ended up as the Mayor of Casterbridge, Hardy's mythical place name for Dorchester. It still remains one of my favourite books of all time.

I ramble on, sorry, but my mission was to get to West Bay, admittedly not the prettiest of places we were to come across, some likening it to an industrial estate by the sea, reflecting a once busy harbour, but now more famous for the superb television crime series Broadchurch. Whilst it was filmed all over the place, East Cliff, at the bottom of which the body of the young boy was found, is a dramatic setting to say the least. The climb to the top is as tough as its gets for the next 20 miles. I didn't let Rosie off the lead at the top as a (Alan) sheerer drop down to the beach I had probably not seen on the whole of the walk.

The red sandstone cliffs continue for a while, after which slightly disappointing low level walking mainly over unremitting shingle, took us to West Bexington, popular with fishermen and bearded collies, as Rosie quickly sat down with a look that said 'Can I go home now?' Thankfully Elaine was there to pick us up and take us to our holiday cottage for the week in a typically pleasant Dorset village of Sydling St Nicholas. With no shops, or street lights it did have a great pub that welcomed dogs, served great beer and food, and the service wasn't bad either.

Day 49. This was to see us walk the 7 miles from Lulworth Cove to Kimmeridge Bay, almost totally through the Lulworth Army Firing Range. It is often said, and quite rightly, that the weather is what the weather is. To date over the many years, undoubtedly we had been blessed with superb walking weather, with only the occasional rainy period. Without doubt, as a coastal walk in this part of the country, the prevailing winds worked to our advantage and any bad weather soon seen to blow over. Except for this day in July, where there was no wind, sun or brightness in the sky. Just mist, rain and more mist. Unfortunately we mist, sorry missed, some awesome scenery.

Beardies have no problem with bad weather. The origin of the breed saw them as working dogs, being cattle and sheep herders in the Highlands of Scotland. Hence their thick, long and shaggy coat. They are very friendly, loving and loyal dogs and great with children. I also have read they have a good sense of humour. However, I am not familiar with Rosie telling any jokes. In fact, she can be quite dogmatic at times.

They are certainly not gun dogs, and renowned also for their very sensitive hearing, the sound of bird scarers firing off in the fields around us at home often sends Rosie rushing for cover inside the house. And seeing the sign, that we were allowed onto the firing range this day, Rosie looked up to me with an expression that clearly said: 'You must be joking'.

Instructions were clear that we had to keep to the yellow post markers, as deviating meant that we could be walking over unexploded ordnance that lay about the area. About half an hour into the walk, with the mist descending it was difficult even to see these markers, and with visibility down to about three yards, I had one of those moments which I had experienced on the Pennine Way in similar circumstances, thinking 'This is supposed to be for pleasure...why am I doing this?' A little further on, came one of those moments that I hear about once a year........Rosie barked!!

Strange as it may sound to you, I do have a dog that rarely barks. I guess the equivalent must be having a goldfish that doesn't swim, and thinking of it, I once had a hamster (called Adolf) that wouldn't go in its wheel. It was then that out of the mist loomed a tank, with its gun facing straight at us, and two walkers, albeit innocently walking towards us. The area is endowed with all things military, both past and present, including I am led to believe, forts from the Iron-age, also used by the Romans, and some World War II gun emplacements. Rosie was certainly not impressed, hence her exultation.

The walk itself saw two very steep climbs, one long but gentle and allegedly some superb views over Brandy Bay and Hobarrow Bay. Certainly a dramatic coastline I am led to believe of white cliffs and darker coloured coves, my pictures of the day are bleak, and feature a pretty forlorn looking beardie who was obviously having a holiday she would always remember.

In a funny sort of way I had started to miss the company of the good Bishop. I hadn't spoken to anyone since being dropped off, and whilst I had spoken to Rosie a lot, like you do, there was not a lot coming back. Bish is very attentive, and whilst banking stories had for many years been condemned to the vaults of time, there was always lots to share about things in life, and not surprisingly the different lives we were leading. Then, almost on cue, I came across a human being, on the top of the hill looking towards the sea in the gloom that typified this day. Seemingly a thoroughly decent chap, complete with binoculars, he advised that he was checking, as best he could, some young persons on the Duke of Edinburgh's Award scheme, who had spent the Saturday night 'somewhere' in this area. Naturally we also talked about the weather.

As I approached my destination I could see three young persons, and clearly, with maps to hand, they were in dispute as to which way to go. Definitely of the female variety, I ended up following them joining them at a stile as we met the main road. Over which, not wishing to let go of my prized pedigree beardie, I ended up, for the second time on the walk, falling off the coastal path, this time into a ditch up to my waist. Much ado about nothing, and clearly embarrassed, the girls were all over me (literally, of course) as there must have been something in their adventure about helping people in distress. Mouth to mouth resuscitation, on this occasion, would have been highly welcomed by this old pensioner, but regretfully not needed, as I soon rose to the occasion.

A day I was not sorry to finish, and one of which I feel I missed so much.

Day 50. I was now back to something like chronological order, in having to get to Ferry Bridge, and from West Bexington, a 14 mile stretch, and during which I would be introduced to the 'delights' of Chesil Beach, of which I had heard and read so much.

A pretty average start, with weather to match, it was a bit of a slog to the Swannery at Abbotsbury, where up to over 500 mute swans can be seen and enjoyed in a superb setting. A legacy of the local powerful Benedictine Abbey in the Middle

Ages, the monks slaughtered the swans for meat. However, you could still have swan burgers and french fries in the café in the Visitor Centre. I jest of course.

For the next few miles we headed inland away from the sea, before heading back towards it, that being the theory, although for the rest of the day, and this is a coastal path I was led to believe, I hardly saw the sea at all. The reason was that I had chosen to follow the shoreline of the landlocked Fleet, a lagoon full, I later read, of flapping feathery frequenters. Guess that meant birds, of which I hardly saw any, but what I experienced were sites of dilapidated huts and jetties, flat fields, a holiday farm, part of a racecourse, a rifle range, an army training centre, numerous caravan parks and an amusement arcade. I made this last one up, sorry, but in truth I would have rather walked ten times round the Trafford Centre, and that is saying something if you know me.

My view of the sea had of course been obscured by Chesil Beach, at times more than 40ft high in places. Experts in coastal geology remain undecided about its dramatic formation and how the pebbles which form this immense bank of shingle are automatically graded, as they become bigger and bigger towards the east. I read that it contains 180 billion (yes billion) pebbles in total....and you know what I am going to say next so I won't!

I could have avoided the misery of The Fleet and joined the Beach and walked the 10 miles along it to Ferry Bridge, except for the following reasons:

1. *It is not possible to get off it before reaching Ferry Bridge*
2. *It is extremely hard going and slow walking*
3. *It would have been extremely hard work for Rosie with her paws*
4. *There are no pubs en route...in fact there's nothing at all*

5. *We could have been shot at from the Chickerell Rifle Range nearby*
6. *It's closed anyway between May and August for the bird nesting season.*

Which all makes my walk along the Fleet extremely rewarding and you can ignore my previous comments. And at our destination, would you believe, Bish had a second home. As we arrived at the car park of the pub, which was well and truly closed, who should meet us but the one and only lady from MB Taxis. Another day ticked off, enough said. Tomorrow was another day.

Day 51. "And now for something completely different", some of you may recall is from Monty Python's Flying Circus. Some sketches were brilliant, like the Dead Parrot One (which was filmed in Bolton) others pretty poor I often thought, but on this special day, that aside, the coastal walk became a *circular* walk, and Bish joined me. Joking apart it was always the intention that he would, especially as his static caravan was sited in Ferry Bridge, overlooking Chesil Beach. Home from home, he was tour guide for the day as we were to walk the 10 miles round the Isle of Portland. Rosie was to have the day off, and it was like business as usual.

The purist will tell you, and I have to agree, Portland is not an island as it is linked to Ferry Bridge by a causeway, which runs parallel with Chesil Beach, but having said that, different it certainly is, not only from the rest of Dorset but the rest of the Coastal Path. Basically a big block of limestone, many quarries there have produced the famously known Portland Stone used in the building of the likes of Buckingham Palace and St Paul's Cathedral. It is also home to a prison, so I felt very much at home and a Young Offenders Institution and to its north, around Fortuneswell, certainly a lot of housing and other development.

With the Bish very much in charge, we were to walk our way down the eastern side as you look at the map, perfect for a man with a left eye that works, and down to the tip at that well known location of Portland Bill. It was fairly easy going, albeit on rocky surfaces, and with some great views across the Channel to Cherbourg on the French coast. The beauty of coastal walking, and sorry if I have said this before, is that you can turn a corner and be faced with a stunning view, often involving a cove, varying in size from a few yards wide, to several miles long, sand, pebbles or both, natural rock foundations, and probably as stunning now as hundreds of years ago. "Let me show you my daughter's favourite cove" Bish exhorted, as we turned momentarily downwards off the path. Then behold, it was full of sheds. And I mean shed loads of them!

Now I am not sure what Emily Jane is studying at Exeter University, but I can guess that it is Advanced Shedology or something like that, but there must have been at least 40 sheds crowded round this little cove. I had seen less in your average allotment, and by sheds I do mean like you could buy at your local garden centre. Then the Bish was off to speak to the only person down there, a half-naked man at that, thankfully from the waist upwards. I got bored waiting, so sat on a rock, contemplating the navel like you do, and counting sheds. Upon his return I asked Bish to shed light on their conversation. 'Tell you later' came the response.

Portland Bill was great. The southernmost point in Dorset, it put Land's End to shame. It had everything one could ask for, including a decent pub, a café, a posh restaurant often visited by Bish and his family, a lighthouse, a memorial stone with sign that said Poole was only 49 miles away, an interesting hand crane which dropped the boats into the water, brilliant views all round, and on this day a lovely yellow looking planet in the sky.

But the highlight for me had to be Pulpit Rock, a large square stone, formed back in 1870 when local quarrymen decided to 'make it' by cutting away the arch that connected to the nearby cliff. Probably about 20 feet high, someone had kindly cut out foot holds to make it easy to climb, with standard warnings including a DANGER WARNING that climbers do so at their own risk. That was naturally the incentive to me to climb it, which I did, and who should I meet on the top, the only person there, but a flippin' Manchester United supporter. This I had quickly worked out in that he was wearing one of their red shirts. Football teams apart, we obviously had something in common as we had climbed to the top, but he was about as friendly as a fox in a chicken run.

My comment that the views up there were really great with a lovely **sky blue** sky above went totally unnoticed, so I left him with a parting statement that you could often see the Etihad Stadium from up there on a clear day. Still no response, I guess he must have been deaf, suffering from altitude sickness or just a miserable sod. Bish opined he may even not have been English, and hadn't understood a word I was saying.

Again it was relatively easy walking back, and for the first time since leaving Start Point we were walking north again and in view most of the time Weymouth and Chesil Beach, almost all 18 miles of it, and we spotted someone on the beach, looking like they were counting the pebbles. Interesting, as I write this later, I read of a Baltic pine hut (24ft by 13ft) on the Fleet side of the beach, with no facilities, but ideal for fishermen, a mere 30 minute walk from Ferry Bridge, on the market for a mere £65,000. Believe me, I didn't make that one up, and by the time you read this you will probably have missed the bargain of the century.

And, in case you were wondering, Bish was enquiring about the price of sheds. They start at about £20,000 (plus VAT)

Day 52. Another significant day, this was to be the only day a Bishop was to be accompanied both by a bullock and a beardie, as we walked the 10 miles from Ferry Bridge to Osmington Mills, via Weymouth, a relatively flat stretch until the final couple of miles.

It was urban walking, with Bish again leading the way, for the first two miles into Weymouth. I was last there as a little 14 year old lad, as my parents decided on a holiday in Guernsey, sailing from its harbour. That's about all I can remember, but it is a place full of history, and it is an area I should know more about, having a University degree in the subject. I combined it with Sociology, an up and coming discipline in the early 1970's, and as part of the process I had the choice of what subject my thesis (called dissertation now I believe) should be, and that would be appropriate for both disciplines. Eventually I came up with the Black Death. No t'internet in those days, endless hours were spent in the University library I assure you, which thankfully was quite near to the Students Union Bar. In those days you got precious little feedback on your work, but when I asked my Professor what he thought of my thesis, all I got back was "It's dead good".

I trust you are getting used to my ramblings by now, and wondering where this latest one is heading, in case you haven't got it, or guessed even, but Weymouth, in 1348, is credited with the honour of being responsible for the Black Death entering the country. It came when a ship from Bordeaux docked carrying wine, nothing wrong with that, but also with a terrible additional cargo of rats infested with fleas carrying the plague virus. It went on to kill half our population, and with no records to hand, could have been anything between 3 and 7 million. It is now the heart of a new tourist centre in the town, revealing how whole villages were wiped out, how the Purbeck marble industry had to be shut down because so many workers had died, and how Weymouth became a ghost town as people fled into the countryside. Believe me, you can't beat turning a negative into a positive.

This was the biggest place we had encountered since Torquay. In my book there is no comparison. The harbour area had a great feel about it, and there is, apparently, quite a buzz about the place in the evening, with some superb eating places. As we moved on, it was a case of 'No Dogs or Bullocks Allowed on the Beach' as we were obliged to start the walk along its impressive waterfront esplanade, and past the Punch and Judy stand. Going back to 'at least' 1881, it is the longest running association with the puppets in the country, punctuated only during the two world wars. Unfortunately we were too early for the mid-day show, which usually lasts for half an hour, and costs a whole one pound for adults and children, weather and people permitting.

With the weather improving, the three of us plodded along the sea wall and soon arrived outside the impressive, Spanish style Riviera Hotel, grade 2 listed building, and formerly the home of Pontins, at Bowleaze Cove. Ice creams were the order of the day, Rosie preferring hers without the flake, especially, as I am sure you dog lovers out there know, because chocolate can be lethal for them. In keeping with this historic day, which would end with us being a threesome no longer, I quizzed Bish about the town's unique relationship with the one and only George III of England.

Apparently the King loved the area and often stayed in the huge residence his brother had built in the town. There is a big statue to him in the middle, as he was very popular and well respected. It is a pity he was deemed also to be a bit of a fruit cake (my words, not those of the Bishop) and is well known for passing purple urine. I know there is a joke there, so I won't say the obvious) but both of these are symptomatic of an illness called porphyria. Interestingly throughout the day you can see above the hillside overlooking the bay the carving of a chalk figure of a horse and rider, some 280 feet long and 323 feet high. The king was dismayed that it was in the direction of going away from Weymouth. You would have thought a man in his position would have made them turn it round wouldn't you?

The last couple of miles were the toughest of the day, with a bit of meandering and a few climbs, the last one of which Rosie didn't seem to enjoy. She had the look that said "It's alright for you humans when it gets hot you can take some clothes off. I'm stuck with this thick long hair no matter what the weather". However she perked up as we entered Osmington Mills, just as I did, seeing Elaine coming out of the Bull(ock) and Dog pub, with a pint of bitter, and other drinks on a tray for us. It is such moments us walkers dream of after a long haul.

A great and interesting day and I could see now why the Bish is so taken with the area, which offers so much. He wasn't to join us on our last day, but next year there would be only four days left of our epic adventure.

The pub is called the Smugglers Inn, by the way. But why let the detail spoil a good story methinks.

Day 53. Our last day, this was a relatively tough 6 miles to Lulworth Cove and journey's end for the year. We were back to the Ross and Rosie Roadshow, as we made our way back to Osmington Mills. I was really looking forward to this particular stretch which I believe would show the Jurassic Coast at its best. It was an early start by choice, and there was freshness in the air as a fine sunny day beckoned. Much as I enjoyed Weymouth, it would be good to get away from it all and share with Rosie how the last five days had gone.

There was a lot for her to sniff at, like dogs do, as it was an easy mile walk up and over and down to Ringstead, where there is not a lot other than a pleasant bay and cottage imaginatively named 'Coast Path'. As we started the uphill climb out of the bay, there occurred a moment in time which is not hard to explain, but is still something quite unique and which I will never ever forget. In three words, **Rosie sat down.**

It was like she had seen the hill we were about to ascend, and said "If you think I am going up that, you must be mad!" Naturally I tried to talk and reason with her, like you do, but nothing was coming back. It was like talking to myself. The body language was all there, and Rosie was staying put. Tactics kicked in, and, as she was already on her lead, I tugged her forward and she wouldn't budge. I then turned back towards Ringstead. She was happy to do this, and after five yards or so, I turned back towards our ascent, and yes, you've got it, she sat down again. I tried the process again, with the same result. I walked back for about twenty yards, and like dogs do, this was now a game she was inevitably going to win, and turned back. She sat down again.

There was no point in continuing this particular battle her whole demeanour changed as she happily ambled back towards the village, tail wagging, sniffing away, and looking up at me for a treat.

We were back in Osmington Mills in no time, as she bounced back into my car with the energy of a six month old pup, she smiled. Dogs don't, of course, but she had won. Beardies I think I told you earlier are intelligent dogs, and clearly she had had enough of this long distance walking lark, and in truth that was it for her. Bless her little furry paws. And as the saying goes, 'Every dog has its day', and in Rosie's case it was Thursday 16 July 2015.

Later that day we met up with Derek Tilt, who I had sort of met when we did the Inca Trail in 2001. He had spent a lot of his childhood holidays in Dorset, he was celebrating a special birthday with his family in the county and revisiting places he had visited when he was but a lad. I didn't get to know him on the Trail, mainly because he always seemed to be surrounded by ladies, presumably because he is one of life's gentlemen, is wealthy, and to them clearly a fatherly figure. I only got to speak with him at the airport at Lima as we flew back, and discovered he actually worked in Bolton, being the top man at a local waste paper management company. We have been great chums ever since and he has joined me in many of my walks, both in this country and abroad, and basically leaves me to do all the organising and is quite happy to have the adopted nickname of 'Turn-up Tilt'. This time with his lovely daughter, we shared common experiences like you do over a pint or three, and we laughed about Rosie's exploits of the day, and tried to put some logic into her action, including how we often try to put human emotions into a dog's psyche. Then we recalled how, when Derek and I were climbing Snowdon the mist set in, as did the rain, and there was little point in carrying on, especially as we would see precious little at the top, other than the end of our noses. We turned back. The mountain would still be there another day. We haven't been back yet.

That having been said, and I totally agree, the good walker always knows when to turn back. I suppose the same goes for the good dog too.......Q.E.D.

Day 54. I still had five miles to go to complete my goal for the week, and for the first and only time on the whole walk, this was to be a RNM day. I was to be Rossy No Mates. Whilst the superlatives abound throughout the whole of the SWCP, this short stretch from Ringstead to Lulworth Cove is simply stunning in every way, enhanced this day by brilliant weather. The major negative, however, was that I had no one to share it with, although naturally I talked to myself, like you do, and later in the walk started counting from 1 to 20, and which I will explain in due course.

If Bish had been with me we would probably have discussed the meaning of life, the ups and downs of his year supporting Yeovil Town, the Dalai Lama appearing at Glastonbury, and no doubt HSBC's announcement to cut 8,000 jobs in the UK (25,000 worldwide) which would inevitably see the closure of more branches, yet naturally no reduction in customer service. As for Rosie this section proved definitely to be not dog friendly.

As I passed the spot where she withdrew her labour, I go back to an earlier observation that beardies are bright. She had clearly done her research as to what followed, bringing a whole new meaning to the word 'severe', and she was actually doing me a favour by giving up a few miles into the walk and me having to carry her back. It was pretty tough up to White Nothe (also known as White Nose) a famous point on this superb headland of the Jurassic Coast, and soon along the way at Holworth we passed a small chapel dedicated to St Catherine, which sort of teetered on the edge of the cliff, with a fabulous view over Portland. Bish's daughter would have loved it, as it was no more, or bigger, than your average felt roofed garden shed. Unfortunately there was something going on as I walked by and couldn't pop in, but pictures I have seen reveal this to be no ordinary shed, complete with a fabulous stained glass window.

At the top of White Nothe I was intrigued by a row of cottages which seemed to have no access point. They are indeed unique, previously housing coastguards but now privately owned. But more so they have no mains electricity or gas, running water, main drainage, telephone, and horrors of horrors, no t'internet! What they do have are log burners and a view to die for...what more could you ask for? And I bet they cost a fortune.

Now the fun started. With a clear view ahead of what was to come, the Big Dipper at Blackpool had nothing on the next few miles. Having encountered West Bottom, on the way to Middle Bottom there was a sign to Scratchy Bottom, allegedly the most photographed waymark on the Coast Path, as advised by the same person who counted the pebbles on Chesil Beach. Not only this day was I friendless I was also stickless, having stupidly left it behind, and boy did I need one.

There were three steep climbs, seemingly as vertical as you can get. My mate Chris approaches such challenges with equal small steps, metronome style, never stopping until he gets to the top. He is an Accountant after all. My way is to count to

20 and stop, break for 30 seconds or so, and start off again 'refreshed'. I also try never to look up, preferring to look back at what I have done. Banks, you know, generally do that…think it's called credit scoring.

Thankfully, after about 45 minutes I was walking down to Durdle Door, a spectacular natural arch which did not disappoint, being regarded as one of Britain's coastal wonders. Naturally, as I was back in the tourist zone, there were lots of persons who had walked the five minutes down from the car park above. As I took it all in, I was a little surprised (putting in mildly) to see the two ladies who were positioned a few yards in front of me kissing, and I don't mean giving each other a peck. I wouldn't mind, but they weren't even at a kissing stile. That, unfortunately, is my lasting memory of this particular spot. It was a gentle stroll down to journeys end, and the beautiful bay of Lulworth Cove.

This was definitely a case of saving the best for last, and enjoying this part of the Jurassic Coast at it's very best, it arguably being the most memorable five miles of the whole Path, and although I could not share it with anyone at the time, the beauty of writing this now is that I can share this memory with you. In total, over the period I walked 60 miles, and pleasingly had a few more miles of the Dorset Coast to look forward to walking, again with my old friend, in 2016.

By way of a postscript, in the September of this year I finished walking the Dales Way. This time it was with another of my old (but younger than me) bosses, Mike Swift, who said he couldn't control me either. 84 miles in distance, from Ilkley in Yorkshire to the shore of Lake Windermere, it only took us five years. Mainly a valley walk, initially through my favourite one of Wharfedale, then onto Dentdale, subsequently along the Lune and the Kent ending up at a quaint ending spot, a slate bench near Bowness. A gentle stroll, it was a completely different experience to the SWCP, although Mike expressed certain concern on occasions when I seemed to be attracted to the beautiful sheep that populate the Dales. I did, however, share with him, that if I was to ever write a book about the walk, it would have to be called 'What's in Appletreewick?'.

It was a Sunday, about a minute past 12 o'clock as we were heading up Wharfedale, when I ignored a Dales Way sign, and deviated off towards the village, a splendid location nestling in the valley. Mike, whose mind was clearly still revolving around a multi-million pound deal he was about to complete on behalf of the bank, uttered those three magical words "What's in Appletreewick?"

I didn't answer, and he looked at me again and said "A pub?", to which I replied "No". Now totally confused, which he rarely is, and clearly thinking how wise the bank was in approving my voluntary redundancy, I retorted 'There are two!' Of which there are, and a population of 234 at the last count. If you haven't ever been there, put it on your bucket list of things to do before you kick it.

By way of a final postscript, I must record that I first saw my present wife on the Dales Way, a mere 48 years earlier. I was new to the school I was then attending in Melton Mowbray, and we were on a field study course in the region, as we were both studying geography. We were looking round the superb Norman church in a place called Hubberholme (pronounced Ubbram) which is on the Way, and is famous for mice being carved into the pews by the famous Mouseman of Kilburn, Robert Thompson. I have only ever found four mice, but allegedly there are more. There is, of course, only one Mrs Bullock.

CHAPTER 16

2016
Exmouth to South Haven Point

IN THE GOSPEL OF MATTHEW (24:6-8) it reads…"for all these things must come to pass, but the end is not yet" and on 5 May it was my usual 4.00am start to drive south, and complete, all things being equal, the Path. Bish had always thought it would take us 20 years, but here we were after 14 glorious years about to achieve our goal. As it was I could have had a lie in, as along the M6 part of it was closed during the night for roadworks, opening at 6.00am, so I spent an hour without moving an inch in contemplation of what lay ahead in the days to come. Memories also flooded back of the time I used to work out of Birmingham and driving down the motorway in the morning, the success of the journey was gauged on how close I got to Hilton Services before I hit the 'brick wall' of stationary traffic. Out came the coffee flask and marmite on toast I had made earlier, as I invariably listened to a Leonard Cohen CD to cheer me up.

As it was I made good time once on the M5 to meet up with Bish, early as usual and how I like it. The plan was for us to finish the part of the Devon coast west of Lyme Regis, and then the final two days in Dorset would see us reach South Haven on the Sunday, the official end of the Path.

Day 55. The 13 miles from Exmouth to Sidmouth was a little tougher than I had envisaged, but, as was the norm over the years this second week in May, we enjoyed lots of sun and clear blue skies. I quite liked Exmouth, once a fishing port, but with claims to be the oldest seaside resort in the county. The first challenge was to find a toilet, but clearly Bish knew the town quite well as his daughter EJ was a student at the University of Exeter up the road. Naturally the students love going down to the town at the weekends, and who wouldn't at their stage in life. In my time as an undergraduate at Reading University we used to love going down to Henley on Thames, mainly to see how the other half lived, and in the local pubs used to make a half a pint of bitter last at least an hour. For EJ it was a toss-up as to whether to go to Salford University or Exeter. That girl clearly has sense.

Exmouth is also the official start point of what is known as the Jurassic Coast, the 95 mile stretch to Studland Bay, our first World Heritage Site. It certainly doesn't disappoint the purists and geologists, although after a few miles, not only did the firing range at Straight Point hit us, but an incredible blot on the landscape, a caravan park overlooking Sandy Bay and Littleham Cove. Now I have to be careful what I write now, as both Bish and I have recently owned static vans, but there were literally hundreds of vans and lodges on the site, all clearly positioned so the occupants could see the sea, and there were cranes everywhere, and diggers hacking into the hillsides to accommodate even more vans. And how can you possibly enjoy spending your holiday in an area no bigger than your average garage, and call it a holiday! And yes, we did.

Lunchtime (not that I had packed any) saw us arrive in Budleigh Salterton, famous for salt pans situated here, in which seawater was evaporated to make salt, and now even more famous for me experiencing my first caramel ice cream with sea salt. I negotiated with the vendor a child size cone for a £1 and it was a superb taste. As we wandered along the pleasant front I spied another ice cream stall, and bought another one, albeit dearer but just as nice. Bish bought another flavour, and as we sat on a bench overlooking the beautiful sea, for reasons still unknown I started to 'sing' the old Simon and Garfunkel song that goes something like 'Old friends, old friends, sat on a park bench like bookends.....how terribly strange to be seventy' which Bish is almost at, give or take nine months. Somehow, singing Cliff Richard's 'The Young Ones' would not have been appropriate.

It was a pleasant walk over low red cliffs to Sidmouth, the caravan park at Ladram Bay being infinitely more tasteful than our previous experience, and we struggled up and down High Peak and Peak Hill before dropping down to the elegant Regency town of Sidmouth.

For ease of planning, I had arranged to stay two nights in Seaton, and at the superb Bay Tree House, run by Dave and former Nat West banker, Sue. Nothing was too much trouble, and for the first time on the whole walk Dave talked us through the fire drill as he showed us round. His breakfast was up there with the very best equalling that we had experienced at the Woodlands Country House and at Broom Parc. He also booked us in to eat that evening at The Shed, a local steak house.

As Bish lived not too far away, through circumstances, this was our last evening meal together and it did not disappoint, and was fitting of the occasion. My belief is that when eating out, the establishment has to get everything right starting from how it looks from the exterior, to the welcome on entrance, to the ambience, to the cleanliness, to where you are sitting, to the comfort of the seats, to the menu, to the service and that's before even the quality of the food and the cost. Your food could be great, but would be soon forgotten if service was poor, your seats were uncomfortable and your cutlery unclean.

To their credit The Shed got everything right, although I am not sure about the name. The steak was simply awesome, and I later learnt the Chef used to work for one of Hugh Fearnley-Whittingstall's River Cottage restaurants. I think Hugh's a great personality, a view shared by Dave who had met him 'in real life' so to speak.

Bish, with his present wife, are mystery shoppers in restaurants. The lengths some people go to get a free meal. The Bank used to pay for us when we entertained 'important' customers I recall. Bet they don't do that now. I teased our friendly waitress from Perth, the Australian version, that we were 'off duty' that night, although it did lead to some amusement in what became a thoroughly great experience for our, so to speak, last supper together. The Chilean Merlot also slipped down just fine.

Day 56. Thrill of thrills I was back on a bus again, as I flashed my magic card on the machine, as we returned to Sidmouth at no cost, for the 11 mile walk back to Seaton. I have shared with you the grading system the Association adopts, and this stretch they identify as 'severe then strenuous' with 2,400ft of ascent. I think they should change it to BT, as this day was bloody tough, with a couple of disappointing stops along the way. But in truth, this was probably coastal walking in its truest sense, especially as the sun shone brightly all day.

This section starts with a steep climb up Salcombe Hill, followed by more ups and downs in deep valleys, and at Weston Mouth down to the beach, and yes, you've guessed it a steep climb back to the cliffs. Here we encountered a couple of ladies, probably mother and daughter, although the former was probably considerably older than the venerable Bishop. But boy, with her two poles did she scamper up the hills like a gazelle on steroids as she soon disappeared from sight, with 'daughter' doing her best to keep up with her.

The scenery, however, was truly dramatic, in that at the start of the day the cliffs were characteristically red, but then changes along the way to chalk, almost bright white. Halfway along, we dropped down to Branscombe Mouth, and a café on the beach. To get back to our time in The Shed, in that they got everything right, I know it was only a café but they got absolutely nothing right here, despite a superb location. As I waited patiently at the counter to be served, an assistant wandered across and asked if I was waiting to be served. I answered in the affirmative, she grunted, and wandered off. Then another girl appeared who was about as welcoming as a parrot with a shotgun and with a face, which I guess many of you will have experienced, that said 'Oh no, not another bloody customer I have to serve'. They didn't have my new favourite ice cream, Bish's latte coffee was poor and expensive but we lingered, like you do, as there was a steep climb to follow. Guess I will vote with my boots and not return.

Many people, however, did return again and again to Branscombe in January 2007, when the MSC Napoli was grounded there, sustaining structural damage in high seas. It was laden with an incredible 2,400 containers. The place was soon overcome with looters from all over the country as all roads around became blocked as they carried off from the containers such things as motorbikes, Nintendo games, Bibles, pet food, crates of brandy and thousands of boxes of disposable nappies.

The BT day continued, past another obligatory caravan site, but our next goal was a beer, although on this occasion a place called Beer. Now I am an extremely fortunate chap, and have enjoyed a glass of Guinness at their brewery in Dublin, a glass of Cloudy Bay sauvignon blanc at Cloudy Bay in New Zealand, and even a gin sling at Raffles in Singapore. And to top it all, I have eaten a Bury black pudding on Bury market, and indeed a Melton Mowbray pork pie in Melton Mowbray.

To continue the theme, I wanted to enjoy a pint of beer in Beer. But unfortunately I chose a local beer, and it was disappointing, and not appearing to be bitter, that is putting it mildly. Maybe I should have done my research, as the name derives from the word 'bearu', anglo-saxon for 'grove', which suits the village's location and it being more famous for lace making and smuggling rather than its ale.

The last two miles saw a lot of road walking as the cliff had collapsed, and into Seaton. Certainly not as classy as Sidmouth, it has been described as tacky, which I think is a bit harsh. I had booked MB Taxis for the rest of the walk, which meant me heading off to Exeter Airport to pick up the main driver. Before that I rang The Shed, to book a table for Elaine and myself. "Would you like the same table as last night, Sir?" was the reply when I booked a table for 8.00pm. Now that is what I call service, and once again they got everything just right.

Day 57. This was very much a day of two halves, and another BT day for sure. The morning was for RNM (Rossy No Mates should you have forgotten) and the afternoon we were off to Dorset as the final leg loomed.

It is about 7 miles from Seaton to Lyme Regis, and as it was to be a long day, I started at 6.15am. Not a misprint, I was on holiday of course, and I was doing this for pleasure. Having just written this, I must add that there are precious few stretches of the path I would not do again (and again) but this section will never see my body, boots and stick again. Never. No not never!

You will get my drift when I say the highlight was passing over a bridge over the River Axe, built in 1877 and reportedly the first concrete bridge in the country. A steep hill climb took me past a sign that read 'Caution! Walkers & Animals' (guess I qualify on both counts) and then through a golf course, with thankfully no golfers who were wisely still tucked up in bed, and then the 'fun' started. Another sign read *"COAST PATH.*

Please note that it takes 3½-4 hours to walk to Lyme Regis. The terrain can be difficult and walking arduous. There is no permitted access to the sea or inland along this stretch of the path". Super eh?

I was to enter and walk the famous Undercliff Path, and it all started way back on Christmas Eve in 1839. Victoria was on the throne, and it was the year of the first Grand National, won by a horse called Lottery would you believe. 800 million tons of rock and earth wanted to celebrate Christmas in style and fell away from the cliff, creating a six mile long 'undercliff'. It has been left to nature and for the purists it is a haven of immense woodland complete with varied wildlife and exotic plants. To me it was the pants, not plants. Overnight rain had made the path difficult and slippery and often hard to negotiate, but most of all there was sod all to see or enjoy, other than trees, trees and more flippin' trees. I saw no wildlife, I couldn't see the sea, nor could I see anything inland either. And this went on for miles, and I even missed the famous Goat Island. Come to think of it, I didn't see a goat, never mind an island either. Eventually I emerged from the undergrowth and got my first sight of Lyme Regis, with Golden Cap in the misty background, civilisation and that lovely lady from MB Taxis in the Car Park alongside the Cobb.

With the clock, as ever, against us, we didn't have much time to linger in the town, other than a quick walk along the famous Cobb, a stone breakwater that protects the harbour. In fact I was told by the only person I had met along the 'path' that we were talking outside the seaside home of John Fowles, who had written The French Lieutenants Woman, the film of which features the one and only Meryl Streep in a wild storm blasting its way over the Cobb. Bet she enjoyed filming Mama Mia in sunny Greece a lot more.

I didn't see much else of Lyme Regis, which I always thought of as being 'posh'. Apparently it has everything you could want in a town by the sea, including narrow twisting streets, municipal gardens, individual shops including a proper second hand bookshop, and an old fashioned hardware shop (I love them by the way) where you can buy nails by the pound and put them in a brown paper bag. However, it must also be full of extremely fit vegetarians, as the roads up and down are very steep and there is no butchers shop.

I grabbed a cheese and bacon cob, and we were soon off to drive to Kimmeridge Bay, where I had finished the most eastern part of the Dorset Coastal Path in 2015, and meet up with Bish for a six mile trek to Worth Matravers, from where we would start the final day of our 14 year adventure. This was to be our last walk together as a duo, and it was fitting that the sun was shining brightly, the views stunning, the going tough and, unusually for us there were lots of persons about, this being a Saturday. More of which is to follow.

Described in the Guide as 'severe', there was to be 1059ft of ascent, taking our total to date a mere 113,220ft to be exact. It certainly was testing, and first stop was up the hill from the Bay to the well-known landmark, Clavell Tower. Built in 1830 as a folly, the receding coast line saw it being moved some 27 yards inland at great expense in 2002, and is now somewhere you can stay. There is just one room on each floor, and by the looks of it should you fancy it, and why not as it only has one bedroom, for a romantic night or two with your loved one, you will have to be patient as it looks like it is booked out for the rest of 2016 and 2017 as well. Go to www.landmarktrust.org.uk, but start saving up first!

There followed a series of cliffs, some with quite sheer faces, and the steepest being the imaginatively named Houns-tout Cliff, with some dangerous terrain below it around Chapman's Pool. Referred to as being particularly remote, there were walkers everywhere and some runners as well. I challenged some at a particular point, and learnt that this was a big charity day, and they were taking part in a marathon walking day of 26 miles and a bit in the area. It made our 6 miles look pretty putrid I guess, but I was glad (and pretty knackered I may add) when we turned inland. I knew there was a pub in Worth Matravers, and I reviewed with Bish whether it would be open on a Saturday afternoon, being situated in a particularly isolated part of the county. Unlike me, I went for the negative, on the basis I would be delighted to be wrong. And wrong I was, but The Square and Compass, as it is known, was absolutely heaving, with bodies everywhere, living that is. We had not twigged the connection with those taking part in the charity marathon. Undeterred where vital refreshment is needed I entered the pub, which doubles up as a fossil museum would you believe, and drinks were being served through a hatch, with a long queue at least 10 persons deep. I decided, reluctantly I may add, not to join.

So that was that, as were driven back to Kimmeridge Bay where there was some compensation in me having a caramel and sea salt ice cream, and the short journey to Swanage, a place I had not visited previously. We ate that night in a local pub, which served one of my all-time favourite beers, Timothy Taylor Landlord, which is brewed in Keighley some 300 miles away. I got the feeling I would like Swanage.

The place was busy, not unexpectedly as its main activities revolve around the tourism industry, because the weekend was seeing the town host the annual Swanage Railway Diesel Gala. With my head on the pillow as I thought about my penultimate day of the walk before drifting off, I considered the extremes of walking at the crack of dawn, and then trekking through one of the most unenjoyable and inhospitable parts of the Path along the Undercliffs, to the delights of Dorset again (but boy there were some tough climbs) to leaving a pub without getting a drink and then finding one that served the superb TT, but most of all wondering how on earth people travel from all over the country to Swanage to see...... diesel trains!

Day 58. So here we were, a mere 4742 days after our first steps in Minehead, on the last day of our epic trail. It was a special day that did not disappoint, with not a cloud in sight, and back in Worth Matravers on a sunny Sunday morning, pub shut of course. It was a good 16 miles to the end, at a place called South Haven Point, which overlooks Poole Harbour.

It was special also in the fact that we were to be accompanied by two lovely ladies, Jane, Colin's present wife, and her friend Christine, who happens to be a Doctor. How thoughtful of Bish, as he was clearly worried that I could fall off the Path a third time, and maybe miss getting to the end. Having one's own emergency services to hand was a great comfort, as was her company. So for one day only this was to be the Vic Bish Boss and Doc roadshow.

After a severe start, with us desperately trying to keep up with the young fillies, in what seemed no time at all, we were at Durlston Head, famous for its Great Globe, some 40 tons in weight (yes 40) a sphere of Portland stone which has the features of the Earth's surface carved upon it. And at the turning point on the Head, we were then walking north to our final destination, first passing through Swanage. Described as a modest, unassuming resort, both in size and character I couldn't argue, but this particular day it was heaving with people, many dressed up, as you would expect, as train drivers and conductors. I had told the girls to expect crowds at the end of our walk, with television crews etc, but not at lunchtime. Their presence had nothing to do with this being a superb sunny day, with children happily playing on the beach, old folk lounging on deck chairs like they do, and long queues for ice creams and fish and chips.

As we strolled along the sea front, like you do, I asked Bish what he thought about becoming a 'Completer'. He gave me one of his quizzical looks, as to what I was on about now, until

I explained that that was the term used by the South West Coastal Path Association, for people who had completed the walk. 'Oh' came the reply, as we wombled along our way.

In truth I was happy to leave Swanage behind, being tired of signing autographs and being 'selfied' (if there is such a word) as we headed on for the last 7 miles, relatively easy walking. We soon reached The Foreland and the well-known and pictured Old Harry Rock and Old Harry's wife, 'she' being the smaller of the two columns of chalk that rise perpendicularly from the sea. Almost directly in line to the east we could see the Isle of Wight, and a similar rock formation at the Needles on Alum Bay with the famous lighthouse clearly in view. In many years gone by they were all joined together. Of more significance, however, as I looked northwards, I could just see what I believed was the end of the Path.

As appropriate for the day, we were able to stop at a pub in Studland, known appropriately as the Banke(r)s Arms. Through the local HSBC Pensioners' Association we had arranged for former Bank employees to join us there for a celebratory drink, and we were underwhelmed by the number who turned up...none......although some could have been nearer the end, for all I knew.

After another average pint of southern beer, we left and soon there was this magical sign that simply read: "COAST PATH S. HAVEN POINT 2½", as we soon entered the beach along which we were to walk until the glorious end. I was happily engaged in conversation with Christine, thanking her for looking after me, and indicating that there was no danger of me falling off the path on this last stretch, I suddenly had to divert her attention as a naked man, clearly seemingly having three legs, was walking directly towards us. The excitement of the day had meant that we had clearly missed a sign that we had entered a well-known, and well used, Naturist Zone. And then there was another man frolicking along the water's edge with nothing but a rucksack on his back, and then two old naked geezers, arms folded, seemingly talking quite seriously. I guess they must have been talking about one of Simon and Garfunkel's famous songs namely 'Dangling Conversation'. Bish, who had now joined us, said he thought he recognised one of them, who should have met us at the pub. He felt sure he was called Willie.

Being a doctor Christine was completely undeterred by these awful sights, indicating that she had seen it (them) all before. For me, although I had often seen some equally dreadful sights in the men's changing rooms at Bolton's David Lloyd Leisure Centre, on a lovely beach in Dorset on this very special day......well what can I say?

As you would expect we had planned a special ending appropriate to the occasion, and soon after thankfully leaving the nudists behind (hope that's not too subtle) there was only a mile to go to the glorious end, and with emotions setting in I walked alongside the Bishop for the last time. We shared a few memories, but in all seriousness, it was a time for private reflection. I had arranged for Elaine to meet us at the end, but then I got the call. She was stuck in traffic!

As I may have said before, I enjoy the planning process of long distance walks, and although I had expected the inevitable crowds to meet us at the end, not enough to cause a traffic jam. But what I hadn't envisaged was the ferry service from South Haven Point to Sandbanks and the mainland had to accommodate all the folk who had been enjoying a day at the seaside at Swanage and Studland and were heading home. There were literally hundreds of cars, heading to the ferry which could only take about 60 at a time.

As luck would have it for once, Bish suddenly exclaimed he had left his stick behind as he seemingly happily headed back towards the Naturist Beach to retrieve it, and the delay saw me get the call that Elaine had parked up, and would meet us at the end shortly, which we all did.

Reunited with my old walking chum of 14 years, we posed happily for many pictures at a sign which indicated the mileage to Minehead. More were taken at the metal 14 foot high landmark erected by the South West Coastal Path Association, specially painted in City Blue. True to form, it was a case of Typical City as we messed up our last home game of the season that afternoon.

Unfortunately the traffic had meant that the TV crews could not get through, and had to move on to a less pressing engagement. No worries, the five of us thoroughly enjoyed champagne, strawberries and cream in the Car Park, whilst Jane kindly presented Bish and I with a superb engraved glass each to celebrate the occasion.

No speeches, just 630 miles of making memories. We were 'completers' at last.

Porthallow
Halfway after only nine years

Polperro
My favourite pub stop

Portloe
Simply a superb little fishing village

Blackpool Sands
Not the Tower or Big Dipper in sight

Beesands
A champion place for celebrations

Seatown and Golden Cap
A unique and fabulous setting

Durdle Door
Just wish I could have climbed it

South Haven Point
Still friends after all the years

CHAPTER 17

The Great Ending

SO THAT'S IT FOLKS. This is the story that wasn't meant
to be written, about the walk that I never planned to do
and with someone I had rarely walked with and hadn't seen for
years.

In my penultimate year in the Bank I was in a difficult
negotiation with a customer about bank charges. He could see
it was getting to me, and he was enjoying it. He smiled at me
and said, *"In life you either have Good Days or Great Days"*. At
that time I only seemed to be having bad days and really bad
days, but his words have clearly stuck with me, and I have
subsequently adopted the principle and shared the expression
with many people, hopefully to good effect. At least ten
percentage of our population can't even get out of bed in the
morning, so don't moan to me that it's raining, the grass needs
cutting again or that you are stressed. Additionally, I now
don't do 'old' or 'negatives'.

I guess I could have called this book 'Great Days and Really
Great Days' as that's what they were throughout. Ok, there
were a couple that were not so good, but why let the detail
spoil it. You could easily run out of superlatives in writing
about this experience, so I won't repeat them now, but if I have
encouraged you to get your boots on, or you have enjoyed

reading this book, I am indeed a happy chappie.

Walking is probably the most selfish thing I do. Generally we live our lives with other people always in mind, whether it be family, friends or work colleagues. For four days a year it was all about me. Only I could do the walk from A to B, no one else. I chose the clothes I wore, the gear I carried, what I ate and what I (occasionally I must add) drank. There were sometimes problems, of course, bobbing around back home, but invariably I could do nothing about them. However, generally, if there were issues, they seemed to melt away when you turned that corner on the Path, and a whole new wonderful visage often took your breath away. Occasionally also you could look back, see for miles, and think to yourself 'Bin there, done that'. I am not forgetting my walking colleague here, but Colin, of course, I guess, would have shared similar emotions.

There will be the odd 'anorak' out there who will take the view that long distance walks should be done in one stretch, and to take 14 years is not what distance walking is all about. Having done many distance walks on consecutive days, and the superb Coast to Coast Walk is one of them, 'route march' inevitably comes to mind. We live in a beautiful country, and the counties in the south west peninsula are up there with the very best and are there to be enjoyed and treasured. By walking over such a long period we successfully spread the pleasure over a longer period, and there is nothing wrong with that. Whilst there were changes in our lives since the start, there have been lots of other things that have changed too. Back in 2003 we were both working full time. Colin is now retired, whilst I am still fighting it with every bone in my body, although thankfully the Bank is still paying us, no targets to meet either. I am now a Grandfather (thankfully the boys called me Pops) three times over, whilst Colin's daughter, being at Primary School when we started, is now in her third year at University. But for the walk, I can't see how we would have kept in touch.

It is also ironic to look back at what things are quite commonplace now that weren't part of our lives back at the start. There were no such things as iPhones, iPods and iPads. No such thing as a Kindle or E-Cigarettes or Loyalty Cards. There were telephone boxes, and you had to display a Tax Disc in your car. Our High Streets were not full of Pound shops and Charity Shops, and they even had banks on them, would you believe. And we now have 'Apps'. In our banking days, that was an abbreviation for 'Applications', a document you had to prepare for someone or somebody to approve lending that was above your own Authority. I had an app on my phone for the last day of our walk to South Haven, which told me I had walked 15.93miles and taken 36,452 steps, exactly.

I hope you enjoy the stories that follow, but for now thank you for staying with me to the end of these Rambles of a Rambler, which in writing has given me personally as much enjoyment, in a different sort of way, as the walk itself. But please don't ask me, as many people have done, as to what is my next challenge because I simply don't know (yet!)

Finally, think carefully about what you write this year on that Christmas Card to an old friend.....

PART TWO

WORLDWIDE
ADVENTURES

CHAPTER 1

SYDNEY:
Up there with the best

THE OFFICIAL GUIDE SAYS: 'There's no place in the world like Sydney'. Whilst generally I do not enjoy cities, this one is the exception. It's clean, bright and modern. It is tourist focused but not touristy. There are lots to do and see, whether on land or water. Like most cities in the world it has developed a multi-cultural society, and you may be surprised to learn that the second most spoken language is Turkish. Now there's a delight! In fact the only disappointment was the famous Bondi Beach.

It is also famous for two major icons – the Opera House and the Harbour Bridge – and I was determined to do both. And the best thing about it has to be that you can easily get both on the same photograph, equally superbly, whether it is day or night.

The architect of the Opera House was a Danish chap called Utzon, who won the competition for its design back in 1957, out of 216 entries. Popularly thought to have been inspired by yachts in the harbour, the inspiration was, in fact, an orange cut in quarters. His initial costing of Australian dollars 7.5m ended up slightly higher, by thirteen times actually, at A$ 100m, to the extent that Utzon was sacked, went back to Denmark and the interior was completed by a team of Australian architects, and to an inferior standard is the general agreement. Said shortfall was financed through a series of lotteries, and given the fact that the city has one of the highest percentages of gamblers in the world, in no time at all. What is generally not mentioned in the guide books is that the tiles that cover the outside actually change colour during the day, depending on whether the sun is shining or not.

My former colleague James has an old school friend who actually works in the finance department in the Opera House, and he asked that I deliver her a Christmas card. To locate her I was directed to the building's dungeons, to be met by the inevitable security man, complete with hat, badge and attitude. His friend was more than a little shocked to meet with me, and that I had travelled half way round the world to personally deliver a card that James had purchased in Tesco, and had been too mean to pay postage on.

My friend Malcolm had told me that I must go to a show in the Opera House, and Elaine wanted to as well. There are in fact 4 main auditoria in the building, although we chose something in the largest, the Concert Hall. Now I have to admit not being into opera, nor did I fancy dressing up, as for some strange reason I did not have my dinner jacket with me. We got tickets for something called Raymonda, sipped Moet champagne in the sumptuous lounge overlooking the harbour, before taking our seats, surprisingly near the front considering we had only booked on the day. The opening scenes were full of mime, and I thought this was going to be a pretty quiet opera until I twigged…it was, in fact, a ballet! And for the next two and half hours men and women pranced about, like they do, often to rapturous applause whilst I had not a clue what was going on. The local rag was not over impressed, however, giving it 3 out of 5. Me, well I was just happy that Elaine had understood what was going on, and enjoyed it too. We had a drink in our hotel afterwards and I could hear a chap in the bar telling everyone he was from Wigan. He was complaining about the beer and the pies.

Walking over the Harbour Bridge, the following day, was a completely different experience. I had seen a TV film of Billy

Connolly, one of my heroes, do it and here was my opportunity. Michael Cain has, and so too has Nicole Kidman, Pat Rafter, Pierce Brosnan, Bruce Springsteen and Bette Midler amongst others. Even a hundred year-old chap had done it, so nothing to worry about there then for an intrepid adventurer like myself. In fact since 1998 some 2.5m folk have undertaken the climb.

You have to book first, and as it takes about 3 hours all told, I opted for an early start. In fact we had called in a Tourist Information Centre to book and met with Georgina. A lovely girl, I however was not too sure as she had incredibly masculine features, deep voice and broad shoulders that would not look lost on a St Helens front-row forward. And there were the hands!

She advised me of the requirements, and that I would be breathalysed first and that the 169 dollar charge would not be refundable. Blinkin' eck, if I had been tested on the Coast to Coast Walk I would never have got to the start of Day 2. Imagine our surprise then, on our last night in Sydney when we had chosen to dine in the revolving restaurant on the top of Sydney Tower was sat Georgina, with a young man, albeit seemingly half her size. As they were revolving the other way we didn't see them again. And the meal we had was by far the worst of the whole trip, and we never got to see whether our Georgina was a man-eating aborigine lass or not.

The Bridge is, of course, a story itself and one of the most recognisable landmarks in the world. A company from Middlesborough won the tender to build it, at a contract price of £4,217,721/11/10. For the young at heart you can read 11/10 as eleven shillings and ten pence, say 59 pence. Completed in 1932 after six years in construction, the eventual cost was doubled. You may recall that it was an Australian company that won the contract to build the new Wembley and that ended up costing twice as much as well. What goes round comes round the story goes.

Statistics abound about the Bridge, the largest single span arch bridge in the world. Its sweeping curve is 503 metres long, 134 metres high and 49 metres wide. The weight of the steelwork alone totals 52,800 tonnes. One of its most notable features is that of the 6 million rivets used in its construction not one has needed replacement. It takes about ten years to paint it, using some 32,000 litres of paint. There are 80 full time maintenance men employed, compared with 2 part time on the nearby more modern 'Bra Bridge' of similar size. And the concrete pylons on either side of the Bridge, well they do nothing other than make it look sturdier. Makes one feel better I was lead to believe.

In the year after completion research was done in Sydney as to the two most popular names for children born. It must not be forgotten that construction began in the midst of a boom, and completion took place at the time of depression and that the Bridge was seen as an engineering wonder of the age, a symbol of a better future ahead for everyone. I will share with you at the end of this chapter the two names, of which one was not Sydney, by the way.

It was a beautiful morning, as I made my way to the bridge, ironically meandering my way through city workers on the way to their offices, or banks as the case may be. Little seemed to have changed here since my London days, other than it was blumin' hot and there were iPods and mobiles in abundance, not to mention the occasional cleavage or two. At the Bridge Climb Centre I duly registered and signed all my rights away. Basically I think it meant that if I fell off it would be my stupid fault. In fact in its early years the Bridge gained some notoriety as a convenient place from which to commit suicide by jumping into the harbour. This led to the erection of a high 'anti-suicide' fence along the outer edge of the footways. They have a similar one at City's ground too.

Credit for the conception of the walk goes out to a chap called Paul B Cave, whose initial idea was rejected by the Local Authority which now owns it. Undeterred he went back to them and got rejected again. In questioning what he had to do to get acceptance, they produced a 200 page document with 67 objections, mainly on health and safety grounds. Paul spent eight years addressing every single one of these objections, and in doing so, the Authority had no option but to grant him the licence. Now some 8 years later, and at £70 a time for each climber, it is little wonder that he now lives in one of the millionaires apartments not far from the Bridge. And good luck to him I say.

Such a story leads me to recall a business customer, on whose office wall was a gilded frame in which was a letter from Barclays Bank, explaining in some detail why they weren't going to lend him any money for his venture. As I renewed facilities for his highly profitable and well run business, he opined that the Bank's rejection had proved the inspiration for his success. Always good to turn a negative into a positive methinks.

I was directed into a small ante-room where I met with 11 other climbers, the operation being that we would stay as a group for the entire climb. Then along came Sheila to breathalyse us all. I cannot recall if that was really her name, but she seemed a good sport, especially as we all passed. We were then introduced to our guide Tony, who you've guessed it, came from Rochdale, not that you would have known from his accent. He spoke more like Shane Warne than Cyril Smith. We then had to introduce ourselves to each other and surprisingly they were all from Australia except my good self and a honeymoon couple from Chicago. "Ah", one of the number said, 'the windy city'. How fed up must they be to hear that? And me, when I say I live near Manchester, I get the inevitable "Ah, Manchester United!" I thought I better start saying I live near Liverpool (as if!)

We were then kitted out with grey all-in-one jumper suits, hats and radios and led to a practice area. We had a harness, with clip onto a static line, similar to what we were to encounter on the bridge itself. We all passed the test of going up and over a bridge, the size you would expect in a children's adventure playground. Much ado about very little I thought. Radios checked, Tony led us out into the brilliant Sydney sunshine and on to the Bridge itself. We were placed in the order we had to stay for the entire climb, no overtaking, as we would remain clipped to the static line on the bridge for the whole time.

My major disappointment, I suppose, is that you don't actually go over the bridge to the other side, as I had hoped, but up one side, to the top, across and down the other side. It was a mere 1439 steps and 1.2 miles, taking about two hours with water stops along the way. My regret, however, was lessened to the extent that I was to be behind Leonie from Queensland, who had the most beautiful buttocks of which I was to see a lot, especially on the ladder bits.

We were soon to walk above the nearby Hyatt Hotel, complete with swimming pool on the roof. The story goes that Rachel Hunter bathed topless there once, until she realised that folks like us were waving at her from the top of the Bridge. She obviously wasn't abreast of the times. Robbie Williams was there that day, with his monkey, having played at the Sydney Olympic stadium the night before, and it was clearly him waving to us from his balcony, singing 'Let me Entertain You' at the top of his voice. Take that as a joke, please.

On one tricky stage Tony handed us over to his colleague, called Romeo. I told him I was from Manchester and that he must have been pleased that David Beckham named his son after him. He related back to me that Brooklyn was so called as he was conceived there. Nothing new there, he said it was a good job they hadn't done it in Peckham. He asked me if I had any children and I told him I had two boys, Guy and Matthew. "Why those names?" he enquired. I explained that we chose Guy because we perceived it would be easy for him to spell. "And Matthew?" I replied that to get back to the Beckham thing, it was the nearest we could get to mattress!

We stopped near the top and had to wait a while for the inevitable photographs, so I chatted to Leonie who had a very pleasing front portion as well. She was with one of her sons, the other who was a 400 metre runner taking part in what was the equivalent in Australia of our English Schools Championship. Despite getting a virus he had got to the final and she was dead chuffed. I was able to share with her my son Guy's exploits at the same event, which culminated in him becoming European Junior Champion in 1993, and that we had watched him in Seoul the year before in the World Juniors where he was 7th in the final. We shared the difficulties parents experience when they have an exceptional child. She then told me than her other son on the Bridge with us was 11 years old and had spina bifida, hence the awkward way he was, and they saw this climb as a personal goal for him, as in all likelihood within a year he would be in a wheel chair. Such moments don't half put things into perspective, not that I ever need to be told what a fortunate person I am.

The way down was relatively uneventful, and a lot quicker and easier, not that the climb up had been hard. We disrobed, picked up copies of the inevitable photographs and certificates and went our separate ways into the frighteningly bright Sydney sunshine. I know that every time I see the Bridge, like you do when they are reviewing New Year's Eve, I will think…been there done that. As an achievement, in the larger scale of things, not a lot. But for Leonie's son, 'Wow!'

It was Archie and Bridget by the way.

CHAPTER 2

NEW ZEALAND:
Getting High

Q UEENSTOWN IS THE ADVENTURE capital of the south island. It is the home of bungy jumping.

This was also the place for the young I hasten to add, who liked to be tied on to rubber ropes, strapped into jet boats, slung under hang-gliders or otherwise and do things that would send their parents into terminal decline. The town itself seemed very much work in progress, with new houses and flats being built that cling to the lakeside as if their lives depended on it. And the traffic in the centre was the busiest to date, unwelcomed and too much like being back home. We parked, had a quick look round a precinct, and left. There was a quieter place to visit, and just round the corner. It was called Arrowtown, a bit of a tourist honey spot, formerly a gold rush settlement now lovingly restored to attract tourists. It was cold, and we dived into the pub. It was the last pub we were to visit in New Zealand and the beer was crap and the food decidedly average.

We easily located our B & B, a stunning bungalow overlooking the dramatic mountain range called the Remarkables. Unfortunately we couldn't see them from our sizeable flat round the back, enjoying only a less than remarkable view of the garage. It was owned by a very pleasant couple, Mr Bed being a lobster fisherman currently on a period at home. Most of the lobsters get sent to Japan, and pretty quickly too. In conversation I opined that I didn't like the New Zealand beer. Clearly affronted, he said "And how do **you** like your beer then, **warm**?"

This establishment should have been called Big and Bigger, as everything about their home, was, well, big. Their lounge was about the size of our first house in Bolton, and the TV screen on the wall the size of your average car windscreen. Mrs Bed was an avid Coronation Street fan, especially when we told her we lived near Manchester. The thought of seeing Ken Barlow and Dreary Deirdre on the giant screen put me off our not surprisingly big breakfast. We got talking about terraced houses which she understood because of the programme, but semi-detached? They don't do them in New Zealand, primarily I suppose, because there is no pressure on space. And if you are interested they don't come much cheaper. You can get a 4 bed detached bungalow, with all the usual trimmings and a garage for your boat, an acre of land, and a stunning view thrown in for £175,000 ish. You get English weather too.

Mr Bed asked us why we had chosen to visit Queenstown, and I said, to bungy jump where it all began. He said he had done two jumps, and couldn't fathom out what all the fuss was about. As we left for the Kawaru Bridge, our host jumped into his seriously big Station Wagon with his good lady. They were off to do a big shop.

I think it was Billy Connolly who sold me on the idea, and he did one on his world tour, and in Queenstown. I wasn't too sure whether I was going to do it in the nude though. The first commercial site for bungee jumping was at the Kawaru Bridge, just down the road, and as was the case on this visit, we got there in no time. The story of bungee jumping is worth sharing.

It all started back on April Fools' day in 1979 when 3 members of the Oxford University Dangerous Sports Club got together some old parachute harnesses and some rubber strands, and jumped the 76 metres off the Clifton Suspension Bridge in Bristol, in formal dress taboot, and later repeated the act down from the considerably higher Golden Gate Bridge in San Francisco. These mad hats were apparently inspired by the goings on of young men on the Pentecost Island in Vanuatu, South Pacific. Vine jumping, or land diving call it what you may, had been taking place there for hundreds of years. Legend has it that a man called Tamalie mistreated his wife. Every time she ran away she was caught and punished until one day she fled to a tall banyan tree and climbed up it pursued by her hubby. At the top she teased him, challenging him to get her. Then she jumped. Devastated he jumped too, not realising however that she had tied vines to her ankles before leaping. She lived but not the husband. This led to an annual ceremony to celebrate the event initially by women, with men now, not surprisingly, taking over the jumping, which still takes place to this day, now to mark the start of the yam harvest.

Apparently it is a wondrous occasion. The villagers spend days building a wooden tower at the top of a steep slope in the jungle, whilst the jumpers go out into the forest to choose their vines, which are then hung from the tower. Then along comes the main man, 'The Doctor' who looks at the vine, looks at the jumper and gets out his machete and slashes the vine at the point from which it will be tied to the jumper. The biggest difference to note is that the vines are taut, no bouncebackability like the bungy and when you get to the end of a vanuatu vine, your feet are yanked and your body whips round. On the big day, just before he leaps, the jumper will stand on the platform, give a short speech about the meaning of life, global warming or whatever is troubling him, crosses his arms over his chest and yes, you've guessed it, jumps. They aim for the sloping ground just beneath the tower, which is soft soil, making for a softer landing because they inevitably hit at a great rate of knots.

These brave chaps owe their lives to the chap with the machete who determines the length of the vine. Thousands have entrusted their lives to him, and there are no recorded fatalities. And would you trust a man with a machete in his hand? When you think about it without trust in the world we wouldn't get far, from the taxi driver who took us safely to the airport, to the pilot (or the computer) on the plane, to the train driver, to the chef who prepares your meal. I could go on; and I was going to trust the guys who were going to strap me up for my jump.

Commercial bungy jumping owes everything to a fascinating Kiwi chappie called AJ Hackett, who used to jump off bridges in New Zealand for fun, before thinking about turning it into a commercial activity. A typical 'go for it' Kiwi, he was once a 'door to door sales man' in Australia, selling encyclopaedias, later becoming the best in the country. They say in selling if you can be successful in that mode of selling, you can sell anything, which I suppose includes jumping off a bridge tied to a big elastic band. As for his previous job, you could say he will have been well and truly googled by now.

The Kawaru Bridge, where it all began, is an idyllic setting, situated over 44 metres high in a deep gorge with the icy green glacial coloured river below. AJ and his business partner jumped through hoops (sorry) to get a licence from the local authority for which, of course, there was no precedent and not to mention the research involved in getting the exact type of rubber, pure latex, for the job. Then there was the testing involved before going live with the public and on one of the early test jumps AJ went into the water up to his ankles. They had simply overlooked that the depth of the water could vary up to five metres during the day.

In business it is often said that the best product or service still has to be sold. How to price something where there is no competition, or indeed benchmark, is never easy. They started with 100$, with a second jump free. You could also buy a T-Shirt for $25. People were turning up but not jumping. A friend suggested that folks knew nothing about bungy jumping, and therefore they didn't know whether they would want the second jump. They therefore reduced the price to $75 and threw in the T-Shirt and business has boomed ever since although it is now $150 the product, the thrill just the same. I was to be one of the 30,000 who jump off that bridge every year, and over 2 million have leapt off AJ Hackett Bungy sites all over the world. I guess he is a millionaire now and good luck to him.

Billed as the ultimate adrenalin rush, AJ claims that it is up there on the list of major life changing experiences which includes losing your virginity (to his credit he didn't say your first jump) marriage, your first child, your first job, your first house etc. Couldn't disagree although up until then I would have added 'seeing the sun rise over Machu Picchu'. As you get older you realise that you have less left in the Bank of Life than you have had, and you should do things rather than talk about them. I was hooked, and am blessed with an understanding wife, so I paid my money and joined the queue on the bridge. I felt like I was going into a disco with young people in front and behind me, as loud rap music blasted out into the crisp and pure New Zealand air. We were then joined by a coach load of Japanese teenagers, who had left their doting parents up with Elaine on the viewing gallery. She didn't wave, seemingly more concerned with getting to grips with the camcorder. I was concerned too, that my moment of madness would not be missed on film. Eventually I got to meet the Jump Master, and thankfully he was not wielding a machete as he weighed me, and asked if I wanted to touch the water. Of course I said I would, especially as it was the same price as not. With appropriately Puff Daddy on the music system I was led onto the jumping platform, having been told that they would count 5 4 3 2 1 and then I should......

I've done some pretty daft things in my life, so far at any

rate. I once missed going to see Pink Floyd, and I had tickets that had cost me ten shillings, because they were at the end of Freshers' Week and I was knackered. I once bought a Land Rover FreeLander, didn't like it, and then to compound the error bought another one. And then once I took Elaine for a surprise week's holiday in Scarborough, our first one without our boys. Her look of disbelief as we booked into our grotty B & B has lived with me ever since. "What on earth are we doing here?" she said. Two days later we were back home.

But jump off a two-foot wide platform some 142 feet above a raging river trusting my life to a big rubber band and risk my only good retina in my only good eye popping out, well you must be bloody joking. We did go to the Kawaru Bridge, and we did watch excited young persons, who for fifty quid got four seconds of adrenalin overload by jumping off the bridge, before hanging ungraciously from their ankles over a waiting dinghy. In truth, I had higher mountains to climb, or rather to look down on, to be precise.

Now I have always, always, yes always wanted to do a parachute jump, and this was to be my time. I had reviewed through the touristy stuff available that I could do it at a place called Glenorchy, some 10 miles north of Queenstown. I rang through and booked for the first available spot the day following, weather permitting. Now if the local papers were to be trusted this was the country's worst summer for years, but at least the forecast for jump day was encouraging. I was to ring at seven in the morning to check out the weather, and slept very little beforehand, especially as Elaine was in one of her 'all over the bed' moods. Big G was certainly in a good mood, as the best day since we arrived on the island beckoned, and the nice Kiwi Lady from Vertical Descent at the end of the phone said that the day was to be as 'good as gold' and to get down to Queenstown where I would be picked up.

I was to be met at the appropriately named Shotover Street

at 8.00am and even at that time it was alive with adventure seeking bag packers seeking that days thrill, and I went to the wrong place. Out on the street, feeling lost and certainly out of my comfort zone, I was approached by a gorgeous female creation who said in broken English "Hi, you must be Ross, are you looking to go for a jump?" Now I knew why I just loved New Zealand.

Marion drove the company's 4b4, which had registration JUMP 4U. Now she was already definitely my sort of girl looking a bit like a young Agnetha from ABBA without the sexy bum, and being Finnish rather than Swedish. She was going round the world looking for adventure and had worked for three months for Vertical Descent driving, making up the parachutes, doing the meet and greet etc and proudly boasted that she had undertaken 132 jumps in the meantime for fun. As I was to find out on the way back, and from the guide book, the road from Queenstown to Glenorchy is one of the most stunning in the world. I may as well have been on the Bury/Bolton Rd enthralled as I was by Marion's description of the road as being 'curly' and the number of dead possums she was avoiding in getting us safely to Glenorchy.

Statistics reveal that there are over 70 million possums in New Zealand, being introduced by their caring sharing Aussie cousins in the 1870's to get the fur trade going. Current estimates reveal that these pests eat through some 21 tons of vegetation a day, and at this rate will in time turn my favourite country into a barren wasteland. I have never seen one, other than a squashed one, but they are about two feet long, pesky obviously, and the mothers carry their young in its pouch. They are nocturnal beasts, and that's when they do the damage, known also to eat bird eggs and chicks. Sounds like a few dead possums by the road side are only a good start. In one of only a very few shops in Glenorchy they have turned dead possums into a thriving enterprise, and for 5$ you can get a possum belly button warmer, and for 6$ nipple warmers. And for a mere 9$, and no surprise here, you can buy a willie warmer. I asked for an extra large one, and our friendly lady Kiwi assistant showed little emotion in replying "If I was given a dead possum for every time some guy said that I would be able to open my own condom factory".

We pulled off the curly road at a sign to the airfield, down a dirt track and to a porta cabin by the side of the runway. I was reassured to see a chap in a Tilly hat, smoking a large Havana cigar, mowing it. What had started to be a bright sunny day, and it was still not nine o'clock yet, was rapidly turning into, well perfection…..the perfect day to….

I signed up for the full monty. I could have chosen to have jumped from either 6, 9 or 12 thousand feet and chose the highest, together with personalised dvd and pictures. I signed a two paragraph disclaimer, paid my £150 up front, the lovely Sheila advising that if I got up there and changed my mind, well tough. She sat me down with a cup of coffee, asking that I viewed the promotional safety video, which I watched without viewing if you get my drift. I asked if I could go to the loo and she pointed me in the direction of a small hut outside the porta cabin.

It was the original hole in the ground, and an extremely deep one too. If it was good enough for Peter Jackson, it had to be good enough for me. For you non-film buffs out there, Peter was the Director of the superb Lord of the Rings trilogy, part of which was filmed in this area. I was in Middle-earth country and with cast and crew for the filming totalling up to 2500 I could well believe that this particular airfield had been a bit like Heathrow Airport at the time. On this not to be forgotten day, there were just six of us, five staff and me.

We all follow the "15 second rule", whether we know it or not. Basically you judge someone within 15 seconds of meeting them. They may not have even uttered a word, but consciously or sub-consciously, we judge their body language, paralanguage call it what you may, and in how they look, the way they walk, what they wear, eye contact/lack of it, strength of handshake, jewellery etc. Mind made up, the next 45 seconds merely confirms your first instinct and when the minute's up that's it. Like or not, decision made....and usually you have made the right assumption. Rarely are you wrong.

I was introduced to James, to whom I was to be attached in tandem for the jump. I didn't need 15 seconds, I liked him immediately. I referred to "trust" earlier, and without wishing to sound sensationalist, I was soon to trust him with my life. It was of no consequence that he was English, a West Ham supporter and former banker. As the Meat Loaf song goes, he was a bit like me, with two out of three ain't bad, and I have always had a soft spot for West Ham because they always seem to want to play open football and like City have a lot of friends and few trophies to their name. He had worked for a Japanese Bank in the City in the hope of making his fortune, became disillusioned and being unattached, had found untold riches in New Zealand in the skies over Lake Wakatipu. He talked me through what was going to happen as I got into my black and yellow jump suit and put the harness round my shoulders.

The cameraman introduced himself to me as Richard, and despite the occasional earing, thankfully not through his nose, he also passed the 15 second rule. He asked me how I felt about jumping out of an aeroplane and did I have any last wishes. I said I felt great (Lie No 1) and that I would leave all my money to Manchester City to help them buy some new players in the January transfer window. They didn't get it, nor did they buy any either, but that's another story.

The only other person I did not meet was the pilot, who having finished his mowing duties, stubbed out his half-finished cigar and climbed into the front and revved up. I was sitting looking towards the tail, facing Richard, with James straddled behind me and the lovely Maid Marion prostrate on the floor with her head adjacent to the pilot's right foot. All this seemed perfectly natural to the ensemble, except for me, with only one thought in my mind, a very short one too, that was "Why?"

In no time at all we were flying over the beautiful Lake Wakatipu below, with James kindly acting as tourist guide. He pointed out two islands below, named Pigeon and Pig, but at that particular moment I wasn't into birds or animals, pies or bacon to be honest. At six thousand feet Richard asked me how I felt and was I ready for it. I said I was feeling fine (Lie No 2) even though I knew we were only half way up. We then circled over the Alps and got superb views towards the Sounds and the sea, before returning inland. James behind me started to tighten up the harnesses to the effect we were well and truly joined up, and if you ever see the pictures of my face at this moment, it is the equivalent to that of the man about to face his last walk to the gallows.

Richard then slid the door open and the cool crisp air was almost icy. And then she was gone. In almost one unbroken movement, Marion was off, a quick bye-bye, and with blonde hair sprayed out through her head gear, she jumped out. I never saw her again, but presumed that her 133rd jump had been successful. She had started so I guess she Finished (sorry again but I had to get that line in somewhere)

Then it was my time. James clearly explained the procedure. He asked me if I was up to it and I said I felt fine (Lie No 3). Although I did not see him go, Richard obviously jumped out next as I shuffled towards the gaping hole, with the trusty James behind me telling me what do. I have no problem in relating what happened next because Richard, bless him, was filming and boy should you see my ashen face. Anyone would have thought I had won a season ticket for Manchester United as first prize in a raffle.

With my feet resting on a bar beneath the plane, James yanked my head back, did the 3 2 1 thing and we were out. What happened next James did not warn me about as we went head first into a somersault, before levelling out as he opened the mini free fall chute, which was to last for 45 seconds. All I remember is Richard opposite me asking me to flap my arms like a bloody bird and give him the thumbs up. The film he shot reveals a very frightened looking old man, with cheeks being sucked in as if at the end of a vacuum hose, and having the holiday he would always remember. What I do recall more than anything was the sheer freshness of the air combined with a relative stillness of the environment. I don't recall looking down at all, although I think James was talking to me, something about the meaning of life I guess. In truth I felt I was having some out of body experience if you really want to know. And, in truth, I have never been mounted by a young man at 13,000 feet, or by a woman either come to think of it.

When you look back on life, there are certain moments that inevitably stand out. I am talking about the great ones, like your first proper kiss (OK I'll say it because it is appropriate…your first jump) exam results, passing your driving test, your wedding day, your first pay packet, the birth of your first child. I need not go on, and I am sure you get my drift. But the feeling when the parachute opened was, well, up there with those very special moments. The sudden action actually sends you back upwards until you settle down for two minutes of gentle descent. I was now really enjoying myself, I was on holiday after all, as I chatted with James and took in the magnificent scenery around me as we headed for the runway, or should I say mowed field. James told me to stick my feet out at right angles to my body, and before you could say Jumping Jack Flash, we were down. I sat contented on terra firma as Richard rushed up to me with camera in tow and said, in true Kiwi style, "Rauss, how was that then?" I replied "Cool Man" with no lies this time. I stood up, cuddled James like you do and that was that. I wanted to do it again, and now I know what to expect, will have no fears. Much as I would love to do it at that location, it could not possibly be bettered, so best leave the experience intact. True to Runrig lyrics *"your memories are everything"*.

There's this incredible place high in the Andes called Aqua Calliantes, where the railway runs through the middle of the town aka the Wild West and people wander up and down the track when there are no trains coming. Back in 2001, when I was there, and mobile phones were the size of bricks, the internet café was the place to be and emails were flying around cyberspace, there was a sense of unreality. Here I was, some five years later, in a partially mowed field in New Zealand with no running water and a generator for power, yet within 20 minutes of my feet touching the ground, I was presented with a cd with over 50 superb pictures of my jump, together with a 7 minute DVD of quality that can only be described as 'awesome'. If you can't get it from HMV, let me know, and I will get one to you.

I said goodbye to the team as Elaine arrived down the track in our trusty Japanese hire car. Her journey from Queenstown had taken her twice as long as planned as she had had to keep stopping to take pictures, finding as she rounded a bend a view even better than the one previously. She had no Marion to distract her, not that I mentioned that, preferring to talk about them pesky possums. Or ex-possums to be precise. I was still on cloud nine (sorry) as I tried to relate how high (sorry again) I was still feeling.

It was still only ten o'clock and this was our last day on the island before travelling back to Christchurch the morning following, and there was some exploring to do. The blurb says of Glenorchy "A day is not enough", and with a population when they're all there of some 215, it is amazing to think that we could have spent a week there and not been bored. Besides taking numerous treks into the wilderness, taking scenic treks, horse riding, kayaking, jetboating and even sliding backwards down a waterfall. Anyway to start with, we just went for a walk around the town, James having told us there was an excellent gift shop which we incredibly did not find. I guess he must have taken a helicopter ride or gone snorkelling or something boring like that.

We did a little tour of the town, say village, before resting awhile by the side of the estuary at the head of the lake. A local resident had three dogs who were playfully enjoying the water, with one particular yappy mongrel trying to entice the others further into the exciting water. Then nearby another local resident was exercising his horse by riding him purposefully along the water's edge and then they were gone. Further in my sights was the imposing Mt Alfred rising majestically into that purest of pure blue skies. I felt so at ease with myself and the world. I had no cares or worries whatsoever. And I still hadn't made it to Paradise.

I have never been sure about Phil Collins. Some of his songs remind me of Leonard Cohen at his best, or worst even. If you weren't depressed already, you would be after listening to these artists and that's before you get out the gin, packet of razor blades and crucifix. Credit, however, to Phil Collins for his rendition of 'Another day in Paradise' as we headed up the valley away from Glenorchy, taking the sign to, yes you're spot on, to 'Paradise'. There remains confusion as to why it is named in this way. Some say it is named after the Paradise Ducks in the area, others because that what it is. You know which one I prefer. The area was used as the filming location for Amon Hen, Isengard and Lothlorien scenes in the Lord of the Rings. We drove through some dare I say it awesome farmland in spectacular mountain scenery, passing nearby gorgeous sheep, ravishing cattle and alongside those amazing

New Zealand turquoise coloured rivers. The road turned into a gravel track, and I thought briefly of that insurance as a stone hit the windscreen. We stopped awhile to do nothing other than breathe, gaze and simply take it all in. And what is paradise if you can't share it? In more reflective mode, one can but wonder how the day would have been if it had been pissing down or if the parachute hadn't opened.

We reluctantly turned back, and found our way to the other side of the lake for a quick drink in Kinloch. As my number 1 son used to say "My Dad can smell a pub a mile off" and today was no exception although it was more like a café and I avoided ice cold beer. We travelled back to Queenstown along that Possum Road, this time stopping to take the inevitable stunning lakeside photos. We dined at a superb restaurant in a vineyard near where we were staying, and enjoyed a superb bottle of Cloudy Bay which we had once enjoyed when dining in Skipton, where it cost about the price of our first Austin mini. A superb way to end our perfect day.

Also, in case you are the least bit intrigued, the wine cost £36 and the mini £40, with 3 months road tax thrown in for good measure.

CHAPTER 3

THE COOKS:
Paradise is Here

WE HAD INITIALLY PLANNED on flying to Fiji for Christmas and New Year, but our brilliant Travel Counsellor, Claire from Hays Travel, suggested we looked at the Cook Islands, which through the power of t'internet we did, and we liked what we saw. Despite being given independence in 1965 the Cook Islanders still retain New Zealand citizenship, and thankfully, and of more importance to me, still get all their wine from the country.

This part of the world is colloquially known as the South Pacific. I think we were living in Wolverhampton at the time, and South Pacific was the very first film I ever saw when it came out in 1958. A Rodgers and Hammerstein 'classic' it starred Mitzi Gaynor, and it was the first time I had ever seen a lady in a bikini. Wow!! Notwithstanding it was a musical, and I am afraid it put me off musicals for life, except for maybe 'Paint Your Wagon'.

I have never quite got my head round when the clocks go forward or back, but as we were now to cross the international date line we effectively had two Christmas Eves' as we left New Zealand on 24 December and arrived in the Cooks on their largest island, Rarotonga, some three and bit hours later, on the 23rd. Now that's what I call good time management. The Arrivals area, so it seemed then was also the Departures Lounge, and no bigger than your average village hall. Slightly chaotic, it was Christmas after all, and the arrival of a 767 aeroplane on the island this day was obviously a big event being the last arrival before Christmas. Depopulation is a serious issue for the islands, in that whilst about 14,000 people live in the Cooks, another 80,000 live overseas, mainly in New Zealand and Sydney. That day half the island seemed to be there, faces squashed against the windows looking for loved ones, whilst there was a tree in the middle of the luggage carousel on which beside usual suspects were wrapped Christmas presents, cool boxes, ghetto blasters and even a microwave. No such thing as a Computer as we passed through Customs, just the usual bored official resting his elbows on a chipped Formica topped desk.

Fifteen islands make up the Cooks, with total land area a mere 240 sq km, but spread about in an area the size of Western Europe. They are reputed to be the epitome of a tropical South Seas hideaway, and as the tourism slogan goes 'Visit Heaven – whilst still on Earth' Or as the Meat Loaf song goes 'Paradise Can Wait' and it would have to, as the rain lashed against the windscreen as we made our way to the Hotel. Rarotonga effectively has one road, that being round the island, which takes about 40 minutes. There are two buses, the front of each one having a sign with its direction rather than its destination and no guesses here….one marked Clockwise and one Anti-Clockwise. And they don't bother with bus stops, pavements or kerbstones for that matter. Street lights, where they have them, work by sensors. They are red hot on drink drive, however. As the advertisement in the local paper says "If you drink then drive, you're a bloody idiot".

Rarotonga's name stems from 'raro' meaning 'down' and 'tonga' meaning 'south'. It is basically a once mighty volcano, where erosion and periodic submersions have reduced it to some 2140 feet in height, and around it is a narrow band of agricultural terraces, swamps used for growing taro, and flat land for the aforementioned road and occasional buildings. Tourism generates about 80% of its GDP, the other mainstays being agriculture and fishing. It maintains many of the aspects of its heritage and culture, and woodcarving is still widely practised. In all the shops, what there were of them (thankfully) are carvings dedicated to the Maori God of the Sea, named Tangaroa. Now I am not too sure of the connection here but they have phallic proportions now, and reveal him with an enormous willie that seems to rest on the floor beneath him, and looks remarkably like a third leg. Maybe they should have been more correctly called the Cock Islands.

It will come as no surprise to you historians out there to know that the islands were named after Lieutenant James Cook (more correctly than being called Captain I am led to believe) who passed through the islands in 1773. That's cool marketing if you ask me, to have something named after you for simply passing through and confirming their existence. Rarotonga was in fact not discovered until 1814 when the one and only Philip Goodenough of Cumberland landed there. Now there's one to share with your friends in the snug. Cook, in fact, was quite an exceptional individual, who didn't join the Navy until he was 27. He was born a labourer's son in Whitby and was killed on an island in Hawaii in 1779, where the natives cooked his body (sorry, should have said barbequed) not to eat it but for his bones which were retained as sacred objects.

We were cooked (sorry, booked) into the Pacific Resort Hotel on the island, and believe me not to your peril, it is the only hotel I have known where the reception area has no windows or external doors. Basically they have no seasons on the islands either, being a steady 27 degrees centigrade throughout the year. No humidity either, just perfect if you ask me. They do, however, get the occasional cyclone, during which the houses are literally battened down to stop them blowing away. In fact there are strict rules as to what to do in such circumstances that go something like 'tie your roof to the base of nearby trees. During the storm keep calm, stay inside and listen to the radio. Don't go out until an adult tells you to (!!) Afterwards, don't go sightseeing, help other people instead'.

We were slightly miffed with our garden house room, which was probably modern twenty years ago when it was built. The floor was crazy paving, the bathroom dire and dingy and the bedroom dismal to dark. During the night we could hear the lizards (well geckos to be precise) scurrying around, and we woke to the sound of a cockerel crowing and a little brat next door screaming its head off. Welcome to Paradise indeed. We needed to move.

On reflecting on our trip, what we hadn't planned, but what happened, was that everyone we came across spoke English. Joy unbound when trying to negotiate with any Receptionist that you were unhappy with your room, and even more so on a trip of a lifetime that had been booked almost 10 months earlier. And joy unfettered when said Receptionist had a smile as long as a 12 inch ruler, eyes as big and brown as snooker balls......and she was called Elaine. She explained that there was a party of Double Dutch people arriving soon, but she said she would "see what she could do".

Heard it all before, but within an hour later she said we could move into a flat on the second floor of a little complex and would I like to view. Like to view, when she showed it to me I wanted to buy it. Magnificent in every way, it came complete with a six foot bed and whirlpool bath. It had a flat screen TV and DVD. Not that it was worth watching, with only one TV channel beamed in from Australia and a bit like CBBC or whatever the kids programme is called. As it came to pass we didn't watch any telly, the DVD didn't work, the radio didn't work, nor did Elaine's Blackberry. And you know what, after a couple of days we didn't miss any of them.

Elaine opened the curtains, which were probably sixteen

feet wide, and there was the blue lagoon, white sand beach and palm trees, with the raging Pacific in the near distance. East facing she explained where the sun would be in the morning…and this was for us to wake up to and view on Christmas morning. I kissed the lovely Elaine, this one for the first (and last) time and guess what when I awoke with another Elaine with this view of paradise on that special day…now you behave, this is not a top shelf book you know!

In the Cooks, they are not really bothered about Christmas. A tree and a bit of tinsel here and there and that was about it. To be fair at lunch they provided a most magnificent buffet, we were given garlands for our heads, and bless, not a turkey in sight, living or dead. There was just a huge salmon and a magnificent chunk of ham. In the evening we dined on the beach, and the band played a magnificent version of 'Blue Moon'. We had in fact started the day with a walk along the beach, no cares in the world, no Mother to worry about, no unwanted presents to fret about, no Queen's Speech, no bits of food to wrap in tin foil, no glasses to clean, no bloody telly to watch…need I go on? As we wandered along the white beach, showing little damage from the previous evening's horrendous storm, there was just the odd pesky crab to avoid, and that was about as stressful as it got. I could get used to this life quite easily.

We had gone to the Cooks to chill out, but I wasn't really stressed. There was nothing to get up tight about on Rarotonga, where they adopt what they call 'island time', a form of up market 'manyana'. In no time at all we got caught up in the pace of life on the island, or lack of it to be more precise. If you had a room like ours, looking over that blue lagoon as I opened the curtains you would, like me, have made a cup of tea and climbed back into bed. Breakfast could wait, we had until 10 o'clock anyway, and the fruit would just be as nice and the staff just as obliging, especially if you smiled back and said Kia Orana (Good Morning).

As the sun shone brightly, there was no news to get you down, no newspaper to buy, no mobile ringing, no television to watch or radio to listen to....I could go on but you should try it. Things were going on all round the world and none of it was affecting us. I would pick up my book, or start a Sudoku, and walk the ten or so yards to the beach and sit on a sunbed, and this little world I was living in would just peacefully amble by at its own sedentary pace. I would go for a walk, mainly because I can't sit for more than ten minutes. I could go to the bar and have my favourite Blue Curacao cocktail, or jump into a kayak and paddle to the little island opposite, poddle around a bit, and row back. I could do a bit of snorkelling if I felt particularly energetic. I could people watch, and there were no Loopies to annoy me. This term I was advised is their name for American or Japanese tourists because they always had cameras round their necks. There were no half naked ladies to excite me either (as if) because nude and or topless sunbathing is prohibited on the island. Or I could even share the odd word with my wife. I could go back to our room, sit on the balcony, pick up another book or that unfinished suduko puzzle. Please someone out there tell me why you can spot something straight away when you go back to them! Then again I could even simply nod off. Then there was dinner to think of, eat, drink, enjoy, walk along the beach at sunset, say Kia Manuia (Good Night) and then horror of horrors I had to go to bed and wake up and start the process all over again. And then there was Sunday.

Sundays are special days over there, nearly all shops, not that there were many of them, were shut, and those that were open could not sell alcohol. Sundays used to be special when we were children, not because shops used to be shut also, but that we were not allowed to play out. And, for some of us, we had to go to church.

Religion is one of the cornerstones of the islands culture. Mostly Protestant in the Cook Islands, almost two thirds of the residents attend the Christian Church (CICC) 15% are Catholics, and the remainder other smaller religions including such as Seventh Day Adventists. The lovely Elaine asked me on more than one occasion was I going to church, and the hotel offered a free taxi service to the local CICC. In fact it was hard to remember the last time I went to church voluntarily, as against for weddings, christenings and funerals. As is said in the island promotional blurb... 'the churches are filled with glorious singing and you will be amazed at the hospitality shown to visitors'. I was sold, it was another new experience for me, and I hadn't had a good sing song since joining in Runrig's 'Loch Lomond' rendition in Edinburgh twelve months previous.

We were 'welcomed' by the church steward, whose other job was obviously as the local tax inspector, and who had clearly left his smile in a glass on a shelf in his bathroom. He advised us that we could sit at the back of the church, or to the side, also at the back. I said a quick prayer, as City were playing later on, or had played, as the 12 hour time difference was confusing, even at the best of times. I was then approached by another local whose face would not have been lost in an Undertakers office with the words "You will have to move, this row is reserved for the Senior Elders. Who put you here?" I pointed out that we were merely following the orders of the local inspectorate and was not for budging. As more of his cronies arrived said Senior Elder muttered and pointed to us like we were members of the family from hell. 'Welcome to the Church of God'. Even Elaine's forgiving nature took on a new meaning of well, unforgiving.

The church soon filled up, with locals of course, the ladies colourfully dressed and most with fans, as it was extremely hot. Gentlemen were dressed in shirt and tie. They were generally accompanied by their children, who looked like they would have rather been anywhere else (like me I hasten to add), the two biddies in front of us chatted throughout the service, paying no attention whatsoever to the preacher. He welcomed us to his church, and us as visitors, without once lifting his head to engage in any form of eye contact, before proceeding with the baptism of five kiddiewinkles. As is usual a mild form of pandemonium set in, with inevitably one of the children crying their eyes out, whilst another one took great pleasure in waving to his mates in the congregation.

All songs were sung in Maori, which is acceptable as it is their language, but there was no haka, unfortunately, to excite me. Our Head Down Preacher then gave his resume of 2006, and how he was looking to increase attendances in 2007. Moving him on and putting his henchmen on a Customer Care Course would have been a good start, I thought. He then went on to talk about his new house, which I presume came with the job, and this led to him talking about God, and how his house was on earth. We then chanted the Lords Prayer, this time in English, which of course starts with the words 'Our father, who art in heaven'…and boy, was I now confused. And then we departed, and surprisingly our Preacher was nowhere to be seen as we left the church. Elaine was probably more disappointed than I was, because it was not like that in her church, and I had to believe her. And that was that.

Our taxi lady picked us up and took us back to our hotel. The lovely Elaine was on Reception and asked if I had enjoyed my visit to church. "Wonderful" I replied, as her 12 inch smile widened at my response. I am English, after all, an Englishman abroad, less we forget.

I have always been an early riser. I guess it must be something to do with not sleeping very well. The only alarm clock I need is in my head and it hasn't failed me yet. On holiday it is no different and I am just the same. When on holiday it is great just to wander round and observe the morning activities of the place you are staying in. There are those strange people, the joggers, who are the same the world over so no need to comment much there then. And in the sunshine spots there are the Germans, wandering around the resort, like they do, placing towels on sun beds, avoiding any eye contact naturally. There are always cleaners, of course, bless them. It is a great time for window shopping too, or looking for places to eat later on. There also seems to be an unwritten law that you don't speak to people you meet on these early morning jaunts. A smile will more than suffice. Sometimes you get a grunt back.

On my first early morning walk in the Cooks I noticed this local chap sat in his front garden with a mug in hand, talking to, ostensibly, himself. I am sure we all do it occasionally, but he was sat on a grave. This is what they do over there. No such thing as cemeteries on the islands, you bury your dead in the garden, like we would do with our hamsters and goldfish maybe. But over there the Government owns all the land, and leases it to families, and it is therefore passed down through generations. Ultimate outcome there then is quite simple. No Estate Agents. It also maintains their uniqueness I suppose, in that there are no holiday homes to distort the property market and will ensure, as long as the reproduction process is maintained, and there is no military coup, not that they have an army come to think of it, that the islands will invariably stay the same. There is a downside, however, as indicated earlier, as Cook Islanders leave the island for higher paying jobs and a better education for their children. There were many houses with doors and windows boarded up, and the inevitable old car rusting in the unloved and unkempt gardens.

The chap was probably talking to a loved one underground, about his plans for the day, or something or someone that was troubling him. It is because that is what they do. Some of the graves were major constructions in themselves, with fancy roofs and flower beds all round. It is not unusual for families to put a table cloth over the graves, to enjoy a family tea or barbeque. This means that the deceased will always be part of family life, and more significantly, will not feel left out. I dare not take this process to its ultimate conclusion if you think about it. I wonder if they have ever tried it in Bury, or Gravesend for that matter.

On one of our days on the island we decided to go to Aitutaki. We had seen a few pictures of it, read a bit about it, spoke to Elaine about it (any excuse) and booked to go on it, a forty minute flight from our island. It was to be the stuff of which dreams are made. Now my Elaine, oops, the current Mrs Bullock to give her one's proper title, had taken to flying like Tony Blair has taken to apologising. In fact it has reminded me of a superb book by Susan Jeffers called 'Feel the Fear and Do it Anyway'. A superb statement for an excellent book, although at times a bit heavy, it highlights the paradox that whilst we all probably seek the security of a fear free existence, this in itself creates an environment which denies us the sense of achievement. The best way for Elaine to get over her fear of flying was simple, and to adopt the Nike principle of 'Just Do It'. And it had worked!

The early morning flight would take us to Aitutaki International Airport and we would be flying with Air Rarotonga. Not many people know that Air Rarotonga was established in 1978, and started with a 5 passenger twin engined Cessna. Such has been its advancement it now has a pressurised SAAB 340 passenger aeroplane, with 34 seats, two and one either side of the gangway and one for the pilot. For once we sat together, as another stunning South Pacific day beckoned.

I hadn't realised it until we got home that Aitutaki is in all the books with the theme of 'places to see before you die'. On the basis that there is no such thing as original thought, at a recent Tom Paxton concert he related the superb saying, which he did not claim as his own, that "it is alright to look back, as long as you only linger". Agree entirely, but there has to be exceptions, and our day on Aitutaki was one hell of a special day, and one, like our visit to Paradise in New Zealand, totally magical. In fact this was Paradise Plus.

You couldn't paint anything any better. You couldn't take a bad photo. You couldn't take it all in without your heart missing a beat. Basically this is a triangular shaped lagoon, formed by an atoll that rises some 4000 metres from the base of the ocean. Within the lagoon is Aitutaki itself, the main island of the group, surrounded by twelve coral islets, with each one having its own distinctive character.

The outer rim of the lagoon acts as a natural barrier that calms the often rough waters of the Pacific Ocean. The meeting point of the waters is marked by a constant white fringe of breaking waves, but the lagoon is tranquillity itself. The blues and turquoises are as pure and perfect as you would ever see. This was as purely a horizontal world as you would hope to find, because wherever you stand you have a view of the sea and sky.

They really do call it Aitutaki International Airport, because that is painted on the wooden board above its entrance as you left the plane. I have seen smaller double garages, as we headed for 'le truck' which would provide us with a tour of the island. Back to the 15 second rule, maybe half a second was as good as our tour guide got. You would think he was a bloody school teacher the way he talked to us. I never knew his name, because he never told us. Instead he asked us what do you want to call me. John came the reply so John it was for the rest of the day. And he had a pony tail, but I was, for once, not going to let this self-opinionated prat irritate me, but boy he did. I was in Paradise Plus after all. And as someone once old me "behind every pony tail there's an a......e"

The island was discovered by a European you may have heard of, Captain Bligh, who arrived here on the Bounty in 1789, shortly before the famous mutiny. Our truck, a 12 seater mini bus, took us round the island, whilst Johnny Boy rambled on, thinking he was amusing us. Despite however a regular flow of day trippers and tourists visiting the island, there was little evidence of much of the tourist industry improving the local environment. The houses generally looked down-at-heel, probably because there are few jobs and the youngsters are leaving for the bright lights of Australia and New Zealand. The main 'town' of Arutanga had three shops, being known as the red one, blue one and yellow one. Interestingly enough, the yellow one was closed, not a tragedy in itself as we struggled to find anything of any interest in the other two, other than more of those 3 legged wooden artefacts with their boastful smiles. There are only three policemen on the island as well.

We were soon back at the airfield, and at the nearby Ootu Beach we embarked onto a double hulled catamaran, which had been dressed up to resemble one of the traditional ocean-going voyaging canoes used by the old time Polynesians to cross the Pacific. The skipper, in traditional gear, used a conch shell to summon us on board for a trip on this magical lagoon. We stopped for some snorkelling, but I hadn't bought my trunks with me. No big deal, I went in anyway, loved every minute of it, and was dry ten minutes later. Our hosts barbequed this amazing piece of tuna, with salad to die for, before sailing on to its most famous landmark known as One Foot Island. It doesn't get much better than this. Its shoreline had the most beautiful white sand and spots of shade provided by palms leaning out over the crystal clear turquoise coloured water. Every picture was a potential screen-saver. You could get your passport stamped in the Post Office, in reality a hut, and joy unbounding it had a bar, well another hut, but who cares. There are only two other buildings on the island, built by the locals to provide for the ultimate get-away holidays, where no doubt you could 'live the dream' of being stranded in a remote tropical paradise.

It was here also that I was approached by a Japanese, camera-bearing man. Nothing too unusual there you may be thinking, until he then beckoned the unsuspecting fellow tourist behind me, and insisted that he take a picture of the two of us together. Whilst I am not sure whether said half naked Japanese person in speedos recognised me as a famous English author and walker, I was soon photographed next to him, as he puffed up his body, stretched out his arms, as if ready to commence on some tribal contest. He uttered something that may have resembled the last words of a Kamikaze pilot before hitting his target, and then he was off, after another unsuspecting target to be photographed with.

On our journey back to the airfield I learned that said Japanese person had been visiting Aitutaki for the last seven years, for three weeks at a time. And every day, without fail, he made this lagoon trip and asked to be photographed with tourists, as I had been earlier. One could not deny his choice of venue, but the rest I have to leave for your unbridled imagination. Uniquely, after being dropped off by a beach bar, we were summoned back to the airport only when our plane had flown overhead and landed. Our day in paradise had ended, and believe me, Aitutaki is like nowhere else on earth I ever visited. Little wonder it features in many of the books (every one even?) of places to visit before you die.

Back in Rarotonga we enjoyed a memorable New Year's Eve, again dining and dancing, well trying to, on the beach before flying home. And my lasting memory, and clearly unforgettable, was checking in at the airport on the way home. We were to travel to Los Angeles, then to Heathrow, then onto Manchester. All seemed fine with our documentation, until our lovely check-in lady disappeared into a back room, re-emerging ten minutes later. I enquired if there was a problem and she responded "Oh no, Sir. I was just checking that you had seats next to each other on your flight from Heathrow to Manchester". If that's not awesome, what is, you may wonder.

CHAPTER 4

NEW ZEALAND 2011:
It doesn't get any better

IT WAS AN EARLY START from Manchester, so we flicked on the television at 3.30am, primarily to find out what was happening in Libya. Breaking news was *EARTHQUAKE HITS CHRISTCHURCH*, our scheduled destination two days later.

Our first attempt to get down under had been thwarted by illness en route in Dubai, and we returned home. This was our second effort, and we wondered if someone was trying to tell us something. Thankfully, but not for the poor folk of Christchurch, our only inconvenience was we had to drop down to Auckland to refuel first. The airport at Christchurch was pretty much as I remembered it, and there was little evidence that there had been an earthquake only six miles away.

This was our second visit to New Zealand, our first being in 2006. Now a fully paid up member of the HSBC Pension Society, I had always wanted to return and visit both islands over a four week period. We were not disappointed. Never a resort-type holiday, we planned to travel between 12 venues in our off-white, rented automatic and unclean Nissan Sunny which had gone round the clock a few times, and certainly didn't like hills, of which I assure you there were many.

It's nowhere near Australia if you thought it was close. Try 1000 miles and three and a half hours flight on a jet plane. A statisticians dream, New Zealand has only been inhabited in the last thousand years. Roughly the size of the UK but has only 4m inhabitants, and some 40 million sheep, tragically down from 80 million in the early 1980's. Most of the people live in the three big cities of Wellington, Auckland and Christchurch. Auckland alone houses one million folk in an area the size of Paris. It was the first country to give women the vote. Alongside Iceland it is rated as the least corrupt country in the world.

More generally, you drive on the left side of the road, but it is completely stress free. The natives religiously respect speed limits, and do not drive up your backside. The people are incredibly friendly, speak English, and know all about customer service, and as you enter a shop you will be invariably asked "How are you guys today?"

Our first destination was the Banks Peninsula, some 90 minutes' drive south of Christchurch. Thankfully there was only one bank. The roads around the city revealed occasional pot holes caused by the earthquake, and we passed a shopping block that had clearly been destroyed. Folk tend to forget the earlier earthquake the area suffered in September 2010, which did a lot of damage, but as thankfully no fatalities, not newsworthy.

Jane Cook's was one of the many delightful BB&B's we experienced and enjoyed. I am not sure whether Boutique Bed and Breakfasts are unique to New Zealand, but they all offered superior accommodation, often with more than one room, all spotless, with hosts not only cooking voluminous breakfasts but offering local knowledge of the region where we were staying. No relation to James Cook, who basically discovered New Zealand, Jane had 26 (ish) chickens which laid eggs all over the place. Her breakfast menu not surprisingly included scrambled eggs, eggs Provencal, eggs Benedict and yes, you've got it, omelettes. And, on our first morning (and thereafter on request) she played Leonard Cohen music. She was impressed when I told her I had seen him perform last year in Manchester, and to use the Kiwi parlance, he was simply 'awesome'.

Our next stay was two hours drive north of Christchurch, at Kaikoura, famous for whale watching (which we didn't do) and yes, the boats leave from the Wailway Station. We stayed at the imaginatively named 'Absolutely' owned by a Swiss couple who had escaped their country to get away from the stress (?) The two bedroomed flat, with a fantastic view over the Pacific Ocean was unique in only having two doors, one being the entrance, and the other, well you can guess the other. Its open plan progressed into the orange wardrobe in our 'area' which would not have been lost on the teletubbies set.

The town had a typical New Zealand 'wild west' feel about it, and like you do on holiday, I needed a haircut. I called into one of those unisex hairdressers and the kind Kiwi lady looked at me, and clearly not up for the challenge, said 'Rauss' will be with you in a moment. A namesake I thought, can't be bad, he appeared looking for all the world like 'Willie Nelson' with a grey goatee beard. Usual pleasantries followed, and when I told him I was from Manchester I got the usual Kiwi response "Ah! Coronation Street". I asked him if he was local, and he responded "No, I'm from Christchurch".

He had a motor home, and had decided to take a week off, and left the city and travelling north about an hour into his journey, learnt of the earthquake. He turned back, and located his barber business, finding it flattened. On the basis there was nothing he could do, he started his 'holiday' again, and reached Kaikoura. He called in at the hairdressers where I was sat, and asked for work. "Start tomorrow" was the reply, which he did, and I was his first customer! He went on to tell me then that he had his own rock 'n roll band too. What a star! After spending half an hour on my hair (usually five minutes tops) he presented me with a request for the equivalent of six pounds. I would have paid double that for his story alone.

Next stop, clearly the highlight of our stay, was a visit to the Marlborough region, purveyors of the finest Sauvignon Blanc in the whole universe. We stayed on a vineyard, and our delightful (but occasionally dizzy) hostess advised that we could not stay in the house she had allocated for us because she had let it to 'some evacuees from Christchurch'. But not to worry, we could have her house, which was of mansion proportions, whilst she stayed with her boyfriend in Blenheim. After being shown round she left us to it. "What about a key?" I said. "Oh, I don't bother" came the reply and she didn't. We were told we could sleep in her bedroom, which came complete with some sex manuals on the bookshelf. These Kiwis think of everything!

The evacuees were in fact an English couple, who were now on their second earthquake, and had had enough, so were going to sell up and go home. She was a lovely Essex girl, whilst he was a miserable Manchester United fan, and with a young family I could sort of understand their reasoning but conversely I just wish we had found New Zealand twenty years ago. They don't want pensioners moving in now I assure you.

Having visited the Cloudy Bay vineyard, and purchased three bottles and a tee shirt for £68, the day following we achieved a long held ambition in drinking a glass of Cloudy Bay at Cloudy Bay itself, where we had our picture taken, almost inevitably, by a chap from Christchurch who was getting away from it all.

When we got back to our 'house', whilst Elaine rested, I borrowed our hostess's bike and went out to visit the vineyards. The area benefits from lots of sun, cool nights, low autumn rain and free draining alluvial soils, to the extent that there are 135 vineyards in Marlborough, of which 38 are open to the public. I made it to two of them.

In Nelson we had our worst experience at a B&B (certainly not BB&B) staying in the honeymoon suite (oh yes) with the en suite area no bigger than you would find in your average caravan, and the over fussy landlady giving us the evacuation procedures, and a six-page guest folder of 'do's and don'ts.' On appropriately named Golden Bay, to the extreme north west of South Island, we stayed at a posh beach house, and the owner was from Bolton, where I spent most of my banking days. Our visit to the west coast saw us stay in a tree house, from where you could have seen the Tasman Sea, if the trees had stopped growing that is.

North Island was manic compared with the peacefulness of 'motorwayless' South Island, as we subsequently got lost negotiating the Auckland suburbs, but we were rewarded by our extended stay in Whangarei, at Brantomevilla, the home of Valerie (ex Midland Bank Card Services) and Roger, a smashing Cockney couple who had met in an Essex nightclub, like you do. Promoting their business through the leading travel guide, HSBC Pensioner Today, our superb accommodation was basically half of their house, with a lounge overlooking lawns, a lake, and superb views to the west. The couple had embraced the special peculiarities of life in New Zealand, notably its weather, its classlessness, the openness and, if you are a handy man like Roger, the lack of building regulations which meant you could build what you like. He had indeed done a fine job. And Valerie's bacon and eggs were simply awesome.

Our subsequent stay in Auckland, thankfully short, saw us stay at the diabolical Copthorne Harbour Hotel, whose bar closed at 9.00 pm on Saturday night. I did have the opportunity however, to walk round the Auckland Tower, from where the hotel looked just as grotty.

The tower is the iconic landmark of the whole city, and is 1076 feet high, essentially an observation and telecommunications tower, complete with restaurants and cafes. Its attraction to me was to walk the 360 degrees around the skywalk, a mere 620 feet high, along its 4 feet wide walkway, no handrail and with nothing but the thin air above and the city below. You are kindly provided with a harness to stop you falling off, and which is most useful when doing the tricks the guide encourages you to do, like hanging off the edge. Unfortunately Elaine couldn't join me, having suffered from dodgy paella the night before. Wise choice of meal, in many ways this particular experience was more hairy than when I did a tandem jump on South Island.

From the same height you can jump off the tower, and plummet at 53 miles an hour to the bottom. Reportedly completely safe, and utterly unforgettable, they provide you with a guide cable controlled to prevent you colliding with the tower in case of wind gusts. As I needed to get back for lunch I passed this opportunity by, and missed out on another certificate of achievement.

We welcomed the peacefulness of the superb Coromondel Peninsula, especially Hot Water Beach at Hahei, where you can dig your own sauna. Our gentle hostess was an Aussie lady who had left their five acre 'fun farm' in Melbourne, to live in their small house (which they don't do in New Zealand by the way) so that her kiwi husband could be near his daughter, who subsequently they never see. Heard that one before?

Napier, rebuilt in Art Deco style after the earthquake in 1932, was an extremely worthwhile visit but too short, our holiday finishing in Rotorua, which you smell before you see, being famous for its hot and stinky geysers. Our final BB&B being owned by a couple from Yorkshire, who kept alpacas in the garden, was as 'good as gold', and they even provided a complimentary bottle of Cloudy Bay 'sav' in the fridge in our room for us.

And you wonder why I just love New Zealand.

Sydney Harbour Bridge

Banks Peninsula, New Zealand

Cloudy Bay, New Zealand

Sky diving over Lake Wakatipo, New Zealand

Lake Pukaki, New Zealand

Aitutaki, Cook Islands

Lake Louise, Canada

Glacier Bay, Alaska

CHAPTER 5

CANADA:
Mountains and Big Tips

WHY CANADA? I guess for many good reasons, on the basis:- it is not too far away, we hadn't been there before, they spoke English (of a sort) and there were lots of mountains to the west where we were headed. Additionally, every one we had spoken to about the country loved it. What I hadn't appreciated, and will be sharing with you later, it was BIG, and that didn't just apply to those magnificent mountain ranges of British Columbia.

Mainly to avoid the Heathrow factor we were able to fly from Manchester using that well known award winning Montreal based airline I had never heard of, namely Transat Air. Also seemingly they are famous for their Unique Selling Point (USP) in that unlike any other airline no tickets can be refunded or exchanged up to 45 days prior to departure. And whilst their onboard service was efficient rather than memorable, what I do recall is that wine was served in 100ml glasses. What's that all about, or is it a genuine case to have a good old wine?

Our adventure was to see us flying to Calgary, visiting Banff, Lake Louise and Jasper before catching the Rocky Mountaineer to Vancouver before joining a 7 day cruise to Alaska. Back to Vancouver for a few days and home. It was definitely a case of 'Trains and Boats and Planes'. Have to admit I couldn't remember who sang it until I looked it up. A Burt Bacharach song, it was first sung by Billy J Kramer and the Dakotas, rose to No. 12 in the Charts, and proved to be their swan song at the end of the day.

Besides continually asking for my wine glass to be filled, my lasting memory of our flight over was the bit over Hudson Bay, which I recall from my geography studies. What I appreciated this time, however, was how big it was. We seemed to be flying for hours over it. In fact it covers some 470,000 sq miles, and you could put England into it five times if you get into jigsaw mode.

Whilst on the factual theme about the country, being the second largest country in the world after Russia, it has the world's longest coastline. Its population of some 35 million compares amazingly modestly to the UK's 64m, and 75% of them live within a hundred miles of the border with the USA. This will explain the heavy American influence we encountered on our travels, and 80% of their trade is with the States.

The Americans have, in fact, invaded Canada twice but what concerns the Canadians most (besides them calling them soft hearted tree huggers) is the increasingly thirsty United States coming after Canada's greatest natural resource, namely water. As climate change kicks in, and U.S. rivers run dry, the Canadians are increasingly concerned that water may become a major bilateral issue and they will be helpless to prevent Canadian rivers being drained by their noisy neighbours.

And, if you are the least bit interested, Canada is not only the home to 55,000 species of insects, but, by way of no connection, the Blackberry was invented in Montreal. They also gave us Neil Young, who has been involved in more albums than I have years on this earth, and Leonard Cohen. I was introduced to Leonard's music as a student, and if you ever wanted a recipe for depression I would put on one of his records, and get out a bottle of gin and a packet of razor blades. His songs are generally about sex, religion or about something you have not got a clue what he is on about.

I am reminded also to share with you that the fine singer, Michael Bubble (!) was born in Vancouver, and he burst onto the music scene at the turn of the century.

We didn't see much of Calgary, other than the airport where our coach met us to take us to Banff. To our left was the enormity of the Rockies as we headed north in brilliant sunshine. What struck us also was the size of the vehicles being driven, mainly seemingly pick-ups the size of our first house in Bolton, and driven in a polite and non-threatening manner. No road rage or a white van driver in sight!

Banff is in fact the highest town in Canada, at 4,537ft higher than our own Ben Nevis, and the name is derived from Banffshire in Scotland, where two of the original directors of the Canadian Pacific were born. Mountains rising to almost 12,000 ft surrounded it in a stunning way, the town itself containing the usual range of tourist shops and eating houses. Not a pound shop or charity shop in sight, and many advertising for staff.

On our first day there, being the loyal husband I am, I left Elaine to her own devices in search of adventure on a gondola. She wants to go on one in Venice one day, but I remain bemused that these capsules can go up mountains on bits of wire and have been known to swing about occasionally in the wind. The one in Banff I decided to walk to from our hotel, and having taken a short cut through some woods immediately got lost, and after about an hour and half eventually found it, and a long queue. Fortunately I had bought a ticket at my hotel, and some 3,000ft later was on the top of Sulphur Mountain with awesome views along the Rockies and over Banff. With more good fortune I was able to pop on a bus back to town which took about 5 minutes, and I was able to meet up with Elaine at the agreed time. In true style I was able to locate a pub, creatively known as the Elk and Oarsman, drink a very average pint of the local beer and watch my beloved

City on the television win their first match of the season 4-0. We then enjoyed a very pleasant walk along the stunning Bow River, and a great day ended at a local Keg Restaurant.

My good friend Geoff, who had visited Canada a few years previous, had told me how good these restaurants were. I would like to think that I am not a perfectionist but like things right, and Geoff, bless him, is probably one notch above me in that respect. Officially known as The Keg Steakhouse and Bar, there are over a 100 of them in Canada and the States, and we were fortunate enough to eat in two of them in our travels. They are the brainchild of the apparently well lived and loved George Tidball, who died recently. If you're in business and have ever stopped to wonder what your legacy will be, George is largely regarded as being responsible for changing the restaurant industry in Canada like no other person.

Having read about him, he definitely seems to be my sort of entrepreneur. When visiting one of his restaurants he rarely walked through the front door, preferring to locate first the kitchen, stopping along the way to speak to the 'guys in the trenches' who did the food preparation, vegetable prep, loading the dishwasher and the like. He was a great listener, and apparently made you feel the most important person in the room. The fact that the Keg has been ranked as one of Canada's 50 best employers for the last 12 years says it all. And as Richard Branson once said, if you look after your staff, they will look after your customers.

In contrast to George, I was once told a story by Geoff, at a time he worked in the Bank's largest branch in the region, with over 80 staff. This was probably back in the seventies, and his Manager, being of superior status obviously, was able to walk into the Bank, through the Banking Hall, as they were called then, and straight into his office thereby purposefully avoiding any contact with his staff. His story goes that one day the Chairman of the Bank visited the branch. Said Manager, to avoid embarrassment, arranged for the staff to have name badges, which at that time were unheard of. As was expected the Chairman was given a tour of the branch, and naturally spoke to a few members of the staff, on the basis of "and what do you do?". After one such conversation, one staff member is reported to have said to her colleague, "which one was the Chairman?" True story.

I guess when eating out, my favourite has to be steak. Am not sure when I enjoyed my first one, as the nearest I got to red meat whilst at home was cottage pie. I think I enjoyed my first steak when I was 18, at Reading. It was at the George Hotel, and a 12 ounce sirloin, and I have the menu to prove it, was 19/6d. In real terms, that's just 2p short of a £1. And that made a hefty inroad into my grant I assure you.

Now the Keg knows how to serve a steak, and in their parlance, cooked to your perfection. And it was. You could have your chosen steak, blue rare, rare, medium rare, medium, medium well, well done and Chicago, which they define as 'charred outside and cooked to order inside'. Tremendous. How is this compared to an experience I have had more than once here at home, when choosing lamb. Our waitress is primed to say 'the Chef likes to cook the lamb pink'. Come on, who is the customer here? I don't want it pink. I complain vehemently, and guess what colour it invariably comes out?

Which has nothing to do with our visit the next morning to Lake Winnewanka. On the basis this is a family story I have to be factual in relating that this translates from 'water of spirits' and at 17 miles long, is the longest lake in the Rockies. We took the statutory one hour boat trip in brilliant scenery with magnificent mountains by way of backdrop over the glacial coloured waters. However our tour guide insisted, as we neared the end of the trip, that we joined him singing and clapping to a nauseous song he had chosen. Yes, he was a complete w....a !!

That evening we tried the local Chinese Restaurant. A mistake, and probably our worst meal of the holiday. I believe that eating out is not just about the food, but enjoying an experience. The Keg not only served excellent food, their premises outside and inside were perfect, cleanliness ruled, and the staff were superb. And we must not forget the standard of the toilets either. In other words, you have to get all these factors right, and every time. My favourite restaurant, Le Caveau in Skipton, has never failed in the 15 years I have been going there. Our Chinese in Banff failed on all counts, and in monetary terms, cost almost as much as The Keg, save a few dollars.

And to end my love affair with the Keg, we enjoyed our last meal of the trip in one of their restaurants in Vancouver. Having given our order, deciding to have a dessert rather than starter, our friendly waitress enquired whether we had been to a Keg before. We replied in the positive and advised that this was our last chance to dine with them. Five minutes later a shared prawn starter arrived, with their compliments, as we were going home the following day. Now that's what I call service.

Banff had been a great experience, and with happy memories we took the coach on the short journey to Lake Louise, and our first Fairmont Hotel. I cannot be alone in having slight trepidation at the check-in desk, especially after a few years previous, and in the early hours of the morning in Dubai being told "we have no record of your booking, sir". Contrast this occasion to the delightful receptionist explaining "we have upgraded your room, Mr Bullock", as apparently we had used 1st Class Holidays. Located on the shores of Lake Louise, it is one of Canada's most recognised hotels with over 480 rooms, some with stunning lake views, 9 dining rooms, saloon bar, wine bar, numerous shops, a 24 hour deli etc. What we had been given was not a room with a stunning view, that being an understatement, but a room with a view over the most awesome lake view you could ever imagine, brilliant sunshine, a fabulous City Blue Sky, a glistening emerald lake, with a glacier and mountains rising to 10,000ft behind. No surprise here, it is simply the most photographed view in the whole of Canada. Grateful of the digital age I took countless pictures on the basis that you couldn't take a bad one, and got up at 6 a.m. to take more of the view as the sun rose, and there must have been a hundred or so snappers doing likewise. The hotel didn't disappoint either, but on reflection, almost incidental to experiencing that view.

The day following we were picked up in a luxury motor coach for a day's journey along the Icefields Parkway to Jasper, often called the most scenic highway in the world. Whilst the local tourist board is bound to be biased, and I seemed to have spent half of my life driving from towns in West Lancashire to the iconic former mill town of Bolton, who am I to argue. Our friendly coach driver had driven coaches along the 150 mile route for 8 years, and advised that in doing that, in his mind, he had the best job in the world. Mountains, lakes, waterfalls all combined for breath-taking views, highlighted by our stop at the most accessible glacier in the world, the Athabasca Glacier. Not being on my bucket list of things 'to do before...' part of our package saw us being transported onto the glacier on an imaginatively named Snocoach, and at 1 million Canadian dollars each, an expensive vehicle. This was driven by a student who gave us all the facts about this glacier, receding as they all are due to global warming, and spilling down from the Columbia Icefield, being so important to the northern hemisphere's water that it feeds the three oceans, namely the Arctic, Pacific and Atlantic. We were able to have a potter on the glazier, like you do, and boy was it cold. And to think we were walking on a piece of ice some 650 feet thick.

We did not enjoy our time in Jasper as much as Banff, and

it was back to normal with a room without a view, and as must be the tradition the tea and coffee facilities in our room came with no teaspoon or biscuits. The hotel was a bit out of town, and for a shopping experience it would probably get 3 out of 10. Having said that it did have a Pandora shop, and MB did get a bear like thing to add to her collection for her bracelet and was served by a lady from Chorley, who knew the road where my son currently resides. Naturally she loved the life out there, and like the Brit Elaine had met in Banff on enquiring whether she wanted to go back to the UK she received the response "No Way!"

Whilst I would call myself a reluctant shopper, all shops throughout our trip were neat and tidy, but most of all we were given a welcoming smile by the staff and politely questioned in terms of "Hello, and how are you guys today" This of course, being an open question, you had to answer in more than one word.

And whilst on the subject, on holiday you eat out a lot, and in our case 17 nights running and the decision making process gets harder. And over there, as the days progress, the portions which start big anyway, simply get bigger. Thankfully, in most places there was an answer, in that you could share a main course, and that is perfectly acceptable. What I did find irritating, and that is a mild statement, is the tipping culture, which I believe is the norm in North America.

I know you will call me old fashioned, but I will tip according to the degree of service I have received. And you may recall from our visit to New Zealand, tipping is not part of their culture, but was always thoroughly appreciated when given. In Canada, we were adequately instructed in a local tourist guide as to the essentials of the country when it came to tipping, and the page is headed 'Thanks for the Tip' and follows with the ubiquitous statement 'When you receive good service, nothing speaks louder than money'. Oh yes, regardless of the level of service received, in the restaurants and bars either 10%, 15% or even 20% with no connection to how well, or otherwise, you were treated was added to the bill. And, believe me this is true, a service charge of 10% was added to your bill if you actually drank something from the mini-bar in your room.

It gets worse, of course, in that this is a charge before any external taxes, which in some cases were both local and national, and which could add a further 10% to your bill.

Doing the tourist thing, we took a trip along the wildlife abundant scenic drive past the Medicine Lake to the Maligne Lake, where we took a boat trip to the iconic Spirit Island. Not an island, more specifically a peninsula, it claims to be the best cruise in Canada, and the view from the island the most photographed in Canada as well. Just like that of Lake Louise, you may wonder. Give me that view any day, and especially as this one was pretty overcast when we were there. On reflection I cannot recall why it is called Spirit Island, and looking it up on Wikipedia, they don't know either. I did, however, find an oracle on the subject in my local pub who told me that in the 1930's Kodak ran a competition and a photo of the island won. As it had no name the winner was given the privilege of naming it, and came up with Spirit Island as the view embraced the spirit of Canada.

Finally, our cruise boat guide, a student, whilst efficient in her job, had the audacity at the end of the trip to indicate unashamedly that a gratuity would be welcomed. Needless to say, and I wasn't alone, we kept our dollars firmly in our pockets.

I mentioned earlier an abundance of wildlife, and this is certainly what the tourism promoters want you to appreciate. We are deemed to be a nation of animal lovers, and at the last count (not a clue who was counting by the way) we have 10million dogs, 10million cats, 40million fish, 700,000 guinea pigs and a mere 300,000 hamsters.

Seeing animals in the wild I don't think is our country's strong point, although I believe the Scottish Tourist Board keep very quiet about those pesky midges. I have seen field mice, rats, squirrels, mainly of the minging grey variety although the occasional red ones, rabbits, hares and once a snake on the Cleveland Way. A pretty pathetic effort in sixty years, you may rightly think. But I guess it is the birds that win the day over here, and I have known a few wild ones too.

But in Canada, if you are lucky, you can get to see some serious wild animals, and no more serious than a black bear or a grizzly. Whilst we saw the occasional elk, mountain goats, deer and coyotes on our travels, seeing a bear can get the visitor really excited, and apparently close encounters between bears and humans are on the increase. As would be expected the bear's day is spent searching for food, and I read that the average grizzly needs to eat 200,000 berries a day to gain enough weight for the winter. That's about the calorific equivalent of eating 75 Big Macs a day. Perish the thought! We were, however, fortunate enough to see some black bears on our later travels, more of which later, and as one would expect, at a cost.

My lasting memory of Jasper is slightly bizarre, but worth sharing. Road signs often confuse and bemuse me, like the one, for instance, that advises of low flying aircraft. What is one supposed to do? Duck? But the one that irritates me most is the one that says 'Think Bike'. If this is aimed at us responsible motorists, why is there not one for cyclists saying 'Think Car'. We are often blessed with the black leather motorcyclists on their ultra fast machines overtaking us in ridiculous situations, or it is the men in bright yellow lycra bodysuits on their super fast '30 gear' go faster bicycles who insist on riding two or three abreast down our narrow country lanes often making it almost impossible to pass. And don't get me going on cyclists using the road where there is a cycleway alongside which we have paid to have built. There should be an instant fine, or the bike confiscated! Margaret Thatcher would have seen to that.

Imagine, therefore, our total surprise walking in Jasper, and casually viewing hundreds of the grey ponytail black leather gang streaming into Jasper for their annual get together in the town that weekend. We were trying to cross what was effectively a two lane highway, and one of said motorcyclists pulled up, stretched his arm out to stop another cyclist overtaking him, indicating that we could cross safely. As we uttered our appreciation, he merely smiled as if he had done nothing exceptional.

The tourist thing, in this part of the world, is to travel two days across the Rockies by train, and in our case it was the Rocky Mountaineer from Jasper to Vancouver, with an overnight stay in Kamloops. Whilst again, not necessarily in the realms of 'things to do before you die', as an experience it was great, more of which later.

I clearly remember my first ever trip on a train, as a steam train reversed into Ramsbottom station on a school day trip up to Newby Bridge in the Lake District. The steam it spouted out seemed to fill the entire town. Later, as a bigger schoolboy in Secondary school in Switzerland, there was the train that took us up to the Jungfrau, the highest railway station in Europe. All I can recall is being in a tunnel, which effectively cuts through the Eiger, and seeing sod all at the top, some 11,000ft later because of cloud cover. Come to think of it, when I climbed the Three Peaks of Ben Nevis, Scafell and Snowdon I could see absolutely nothing past my nose on their summits. Later I was to climb the highest peak in Ireland, namely Carrantuohill, and no guesses what I saw from the top. As that Wenger chap would often say "Sorry didn't see anything". The Settle to Carlisle railway line is interesting rather than spectacular, but it was good to pass over the

Ribblehead Viaduct after walking under it many times. And I don't think I will ever do the Orient Express, as some people say it's murder.

About 70,000 people a year travel on the Rocky Mountaineer, and we were advised to 'push the boat out' (sic) and go for the bi-level glass domed coach. Sound advice, it certainly met with their great motto of 'No request will go unmet'. They certainly matched the Ronseal test with flying colours. I don't recall ever sitting upstairs on a train, and being at the front on the front coach meant first to be served from the bar. It's all in the planning, and one of my many abiding memories of the trip was seeing Elaine enjoying a gin and tonic at 11.00am on a Sunday morning. Am sure Big G allows her to have the occasional Sunday off.

Having left Jasper in mixed weather, we were soon surrounded by dramatic scenery for which words seem inadequate, and the highest mountain of the Rockies, Mount Robson, at nearly 13,000ft, was somewhere up there in the clouds (how do I do it?) although we did see the lower reaches of the famous Pyramid Falls.

We were directed downstairs for our lunch, which we shared with a charming couple from Bournemouth, namely Mary and Damian. We had lots in common, and we shared our New Zealand experiences, but how I teased Damian who had hired a camper van over there, and had taken his bicycle with him. Mindful of my previous comments re lycramen, here I was dining with one who had taken his bike on holiday with him to the other side of the world, and I had thought long and hard whether to take my iPod with me on this trip.

Also, in true Japanese style, he had a camera with a lens seemingly the length of a cricket bat. He kindly sent me some of his pictures, and they were superb. I guess size does matter. It also reminds me of many photographers on the viewing platform leaning out to take pictures just as we were approaching the many tunnels en route, but even more bizarre seeing those stretching out with their iPads. Am sure some of them took smashing pictures.

Our overnight stop was at Kamloops, where 1st Class Holidays, bless them, apologised that there were no deluxe hotels, and that accommodation was of only of a moderate grade. No problem, it was clean, bright and with the usual seven foot bed. Known as a transportation hub for road and rail, it is famous for having a crater on the moon named after it. Instantly forgettable, we walked round most of it looking for something to eat, as most of the restaurants were closed because it was Sunday night.

Our second day saw the dramatic scenery flatten out, but the wine still flowed as did the rivers to the approaching Pacific Ocean. I expanded my vast album of bird pictures by being fortunate enough to take one of a nesting bald eagle as I idly counted the number of carriages on a train travelling east. Some of the carriage trains are up to half a mile long and I lost count as it reached over 200 in number. My thoughts wandered as to how we would find (not literally of course) Vancouver, as our organised adventure moved into its next phase.

Final thoughts on the Rocky Mountaineer experience were as positive as those of The Keg, and in their service proposition it was difficult not to give it a 'perfect ten'. What made this score, and I have not mentioned this earlier, were the staff, and especially the two who served us in our carriage. Inevitably it seemed, the young girl, Charlotte, was a student in her vacation period, supported by a chap called Scott, a little older and more permanent. They never stopped, and in between superb customer service, they were preparing drinks and snacks, washing up, and then grabbing the microphone to describe where we were on the trip, and the significance of the particular area. All presented without notes, and perfect delivery. And whilst we kinda (I am slipping into their parlance now) got used to great service throughout the holiday, it is no co-incidence that both organisations regularly win awards for how they treat their staff.

I started this chapter with the word BIG, and things were about to get BIGGER, as we hit Vancouver, a city of very tall skyscrapers I had heard only good things about. We were booked into the Fairmont Waterfront Hotel, and heard that magic statement again "We have upgraded you, Mr Bullock" and 'up' was appropriate as we were allocated a room on the 19th floor (think it went up to 30) with a magnificent view over the harbour. Our suitcases were already in the room (now that's service!) and the bed was at least 12 foot wide, not that I had a tape measure with me, and Elaine had an uninterrupted sleep she was pleased to tell me.

This city, often referred to as a city of neighbourhoods, is the most densely populated in Canada, and is consistently named in the Top 5 worldwide for livability and quality of life. Over 50% do not speak English as a first language, and a high Chinese population was added to following the transfer of sovereignty of Hong Kong in 1997. And I was told that Vancouver has the purest drugs in Canada due to its situation on the Pacific Rim and its direct route from the Far East. Read into that fact as you wish.

We had one full day in the city before jumping on the boat to Alaska, and chose to spend the day on one of those 'hop and off buses' and this involved mainly 'doing' Stanley Park, recognised by the experts on the subject as one of the great urban parks in the whole wide world. Despite the views of my great chum Geoff, in my mind it was good, not great, although it remains the city's most visited tourist attraction. You can walk round it in two hours, cycle round in an hour (don't get me going!) and bizarrely, being a peninsula, has a second beach, a third beach, but yes, you've got it, no first beach because I could not and did not find it. My lasting memory of the park was when we bumped into a couple and the man was wearing a Runrig tee-shirt. Now Runrig are my all time favourite Scottish folk/rock band who I have seen many times. Trying to engage said tee-shirt wearer, like you do on holiday, I told him I was one of their greatest fans. In what was clearly a Scottish accent he merely grunted "Never seen them" and trundled away.

Our hotel looked over Coal Harbour and Canada Place from where our ship was to leave and it was a mere walk across the road, with our suitcases. With total efficiency, and on the basis they had done it lots of time before, the embarkation process was a little more complicated as we were to sail in US waters and we needed an ESTA, like one does, and for a charge of 14 dollars each. What a con! Just think how our balance of payments would benefit if we charged the Yanks a similar fee once they hit English waters after crossing the Atlantic. We were, however, sympathetically processed by the American passport control officials and allowed to board. And with a little sense of humour I may add, having seen my surname, with what became the usual question on our travels "Are you any relation to Sandra Bullock?" My usual reply of "Yes, I am very proud of my daughter's achievements" created the usual wry smile, and I wondered why they asked the question in the first place.

So, for the first and last time in my life I was off to Alaska. Being a history graduate (may have told you that before) I was always interested in the sale of the country by the Russians to America in 1867 for US$ 7.2m. On the basis that you can't get an average Premiership full back for that price now, America acquired a country twice the size of Texas. At the time Russia needed the money, and in fact offered it to us first, but we expressed little interest. The Americans bought it primarily for its seal fishery, whilst gold and oil was to follow. The citizens at the time couldn't wait to get back to Russia, as, like me, they simply could not get the hang of American rules football.

Holiday cruises, I believe, are in the marmite class of tastes in that you either like them or not. Having said that, whilst I love marmite and always take some on holiday with me, I like the principle of cruising but not necessarily the practice. I will describe our Glacier Bay experience later by way of explanation.

We enjoyed our first cruise in the Caribbean, visiting some wonderful islands, with the exceptional Tortolla coming to mind, only to be whisked away some five hours later, never to return. I seemed to spend a life time in my dinner jacket, and being thrust into dining situations with boring couples. Opening question invariably asked of us was 'Have you cruised before?' followed by the questioner then relating to us for the next hour or so the cruises they had been on and places visited. Our cruise up the North Sea to the top of Norway saw us paying extra for a room with a balcony which we couldn't enjoy because it was so cold, on a ship too big to go up the fjords, and weather so bad that we couldn't get off the ship on any of the rip-off excursions. To cap it all we had to dine for seven nights with an exceptionally uninspiring couple from St Helens whose primary reason for cruising was to enjoy the ballroom dancing.

This cruise on the Holland America Volendam, was to see us travelling north from Vancouver calling at Juneau, Skagway and Ketchikan, but the highlight of the voyage was to be enjoyed without us leaving the ship. At a mere 61,000 tons, it was thankfully not a big ship with only 1432 guests and 604 crew, the latter mainly of the Filipino variety. It has an amazing economic fuel consumption of 85 gallons a mile. The biggest cruise ship currently out there is, I believe, the Oasis of the Seas which is nearly four times bigger in tonnage, can accommodate 5,400 passengers, and has 37 restaurants and 20 bars. Here in Tarleton we have a similar population, and have 2 restaurants and 2 pubs, but guess I am not comparing like with like as they probably don't serve a decent pint of Thwaites Original on the Oasis.

Now is the time to explain my love/hate relationship with cruising. Like our previous experiences with P & O, Holland America did not disappoint with the level of service we received which we paid for, of course, with a daily charge on our bill, and every time we bought a drink or coffee. You have a variety of eating and drinking places, and there are no worries about drinking and driving. The entertainment is generally of a high standard, and you will invariably find an old chap playing the grand piano somewhere on board. But most of all, there is something quite exciting to wake up in the morning and look out of the window at a fresh and invariably exhilarating view, and on this cruise, one which often brings a whole new meaning to the word 'awesome'.

Now the pain! I have been accused (can't think by whom) of being a control freak, and I don't like being organised, herded, or having someone slap a sticker on my lapel with my name on. I am told I am good with people, and not unusually have spent a lifetime working for and with people of all types, sizes and cultures but on holiday I like to get away from it (them) all. No chance on a cruise ship, and especially one with hundreds of North Americans seemingly all being big, bigger, loud, louder and I have to say it, sometimes very rude. I exaggerate, of course. It's just that in a confined space, which even big ships can be, it all just seems so much worse.

But most of all, it was the buffets on board that got to me. Their advantage is well known, in that you can generally choose what and how much you want or fancy. So why do our friends pile their plates high, leave half or more of it behind and then go back for more? Pointless providing cutlery and I am mindful of breakfast when we stayed in Jasper and there was a chap eating breakfast, of the traditional 'English' variety including baked beans and eggs, and he was using his fingers! Also his son, who was on his way to being as big as his Dad, was doing the same. Nothing is ever finished, and when they get up to leave, the table looked like a tsunami had passed through the deck or the ship had just hit an iceberg.

It is often said that we are a product of our culture, and readers out there will remember as children having to eat absolutely everything that was presented on your plate, not having a pudding if you didn't eat everything, and leaving your knife and fork in the centre of your plate. My boys were sick of me calling this process as 'etiquette', and in her later years I recall telling my mother off for leaving her knife and fork straddled across her plate in true American style.

To get back to that magic word of etiquette, defined in my Oxford dictionary as 'the rules of correct behaviour in society' there were only two formal dinners on the cruise, and not of the black tie variety, but I lost count of the number of male passengers who sat down for their meals wearing baseball caps and trainers.

Another thing I found bizarre in the mornings, was not only those strange people, all in the appropriate gear, running round and round the ship on a designated route (good job they weren't on bikes) but the other extreme seeing lots of passengers plonked in front of gaming machines, seemingly hundreds of them, feeding them with dollar after dollar. And boy, what was that room like on the days at sea.

My final gripe on cruising, and probably my biggest one, is the shore excursions, or how to be ripped off in one single transaction. Holland America were no different in their promotion, and whilst no obligation, we had to sit through the nauseating sales pitch from our Kevin and his clamorous sidekick in the theatre, supported by the inevitable videos of the absolute splendour you simply couldn't miss. On this trip we had the choice of a mere 100 or so, the most expensive a mere $526 for the undoubted pleasure of walking on a glacier (done that) or going on a 'guaranteed' whale viewing trip or getting a partial refund! And if you fancy a helicopter trip, and weigh more than 250lbs (including clothing and baseball cap) you have to pay a modest surcharge of $120 or risk being thrown off. Also, you get the 'book now to avoid disappointment' nonsense and having considered our options we later booked three excursions, and in terms of enjoyment Meat Loaf would sing '2 out of 3 ain't (weren't) bad'.

We left Vancouver in traditional style with champagne glass in hand and waving to people on shore we didn't know. In a poignant moment you can't imagine what it could have been like for loved ones waving to soldiers on troop ships going to war, and inevitably wondering if they would return. There was to be a full day at sea cruising through what is uniquely known as the inside passage to our first port of call, the gold rush port of Juneau, a place you can only get to, whilst we are on the subject, by either through the birth channel, or by boat or plane.

On the basis there is not a lot to see in Juneau on the best of days (it was misty and raining for us) Kevin and Stacey, the tour guide Salespersons, had had a field day selling us the 40 or so trips to get you out of the town or into the sky. We could, however, have gone to Gold Creek, where gold was first struck in 1880, and learn how to work the pan. And guess what....you could take home all (yes all) the gold you found!

Which leads me nicely onto dogs. We had an enjoyable trip to a Mushers Camp, where they rear and train huskies, mainly for the famous annual Iditarod race, where sixteen of them pull a sled with the 'pilot', namely the musher, a mere 444 miles from Anchorage to Ophir. They pass through blizzards, sub-zero temperatures, gale force winds through tundra, forests, over rivers and mountain passes. This can take between 8 and

15 days depending on the weather, and no wonder this is called the last Great Race on Earth. About fifty teams take part in the race which is run every year in March.

This was a worthwhile (if over-priced) experience, well organised, and a lot better than our neighbours who had chosen the tramway up a local mountain and seen precious little at the top because of the mist (see later). Next stop on the voyage was Skagway, and home to the ladies of negotiable affection.

Skagway was great. It is positioned at the tip of the Inside Passage and is another gold rush town, made famous in 1897 with the cry of 'Gold in the Yukon' seeing its population mushroom in no time from 200 to 10,000, making it the largest town in Alaska, with all the usual amenities of a large city, which included 80 saloons, several bordellos and plenty of thieves. A tourist board heaven, it now has everything you could want if holidaying, with wooden walkways and wooden fronted buildings giving the place a wild west feel about it; and naturally there was a shop selling Pandora charms and a Chinese Takeaway.

I was able to escape with a quick visit to The Red Onion Saloon, once the town's most exclusive bordello and was served by a large tart-like lady with what can only be described as the largest cleavage this side of the Pacific and in which I could have spent the rest of my holiday. She then served me with a glass of Dicks Danger Ale, a very average beer, and then politely enquired whether I would be joining her on the guided tour of the brothel museum upstairs, where the ladies never miss a trick. I politely refused with the excuse of I had a boat to catch, and then studied the beer mat, like you do.

Renovated in 1980, with fresh sawdust on the floor and its historic 19 foot mahogany bar glistening with polish, the Saloon was first opened in 1898, selling alcohol on the ground floor, whilst upstairs more than the prospector's thirst was satisfied. The brothel itself consisted of ten cubicles, called cribs, no bigger than ten foot square. Each room had a hole in the floor which connected to the cash register downstairs by means of a copper tube. In order to keep track of which girls were busy, the barman kept ten dolls at the back of the bar, one for each of the girls. When a girl was with her customer the doll was laid on its back. When she sent the earnings (usually $5) down the tube the doll was returned to the upright position, which indicated she was ready for another customer. Next please!

Do you ever wonder why you do something? In my banking days it was my job to lend money, and when it went wrong, not too often thankfully, I used to ask myself 'Why did I lend to that person?' and the answer only ever could be that it seemed like a good idea at the time. So why did we spend £200 to go on a train that took us to the top of the White Pass Summit, a narrow-gauge railroad that was built to transport the miners from Skagway to the gold fields. Allegedly it is an International Historic Civil Engineering Landmark, an honour shared with the Panama Canal, the Eiffel Tower, the Statue of Liberty and the Etihad Stadium (made the last one up, of course).

What was supposed to be an unforgettable experience turned out to be an instantly forgettable 3½ hour journey of mist, cloud, rain and sheer disappointment of which we could see precious little out of the window, and a tour guide, once again a student, who was more interested in trying to sell us merchandise at discount prices as it was getting to the end of the season, and he was back at college the next week. We got to the top of the pass, watched the grass grow for twenty minutes and turned back down the mountain. The fact that I have the grand sum of one picture, following my never to be forgotten journey, I guess, says it all.

Not sure what you get for £200, but a couple of cases of a

fine Merlot immediately comes to mind. It gets worse of course, as in conversation with a fine lady on the cruise that evening, she revealed to us that she had bought tickets at the station for the trip, adjacent to where the ship had docked, for the grand sum equivalent of £40. Following on to what I said earlier about excursions, I rest my case.

Frank Sinatra is credited with the song 'The best is yet to come' and being a 'half full' type of person this is certainly true as our ship turned back south on its journey back to Vancouver. At about 5.30 am the morning following, our vessel entered Glacier Bay National Park and Reserve, and what was to follow in the next few hours was incredibly unique, and probably the highlight of the whole trip. Glacier Bay has everything, being a homeland, natural laboratory, a wilderness, a national park, a United Nations biosphere reserve and a world heritage site. That's not bad for a youngster in nature terms as only 250 years ago it was all glacier and no bay, but through natural warming the glacier effectively retreated and disappeared all of 65 miles.

And for the first time on the trip we were blessed with a dry morning, and the mist slowly cleared as our ship headed north up the bay, surrounded by great chunks of pure white ice on the water that had fallen off glaciers. There was a certain bleak eeriness around, a strange stillness only stifled by the noise of our ship. Almost as if by order, as we reached the head of the bay, the clouds lifted, the sun shone and the true splendour of the visage exhibited itself where two glaciers met, namely the Grand Pacific and Margerie. Our erudite English Captain, James Russell-Dunford switched off his engines for a while, and the peacefulness of the occasion was shattered occasionally by big chunks of ice falling off Margerie, exhibiting the sound not unlike gunshots. And I have not mentioned the colours, with every shade of blue and turquoise imaginable in sky and waters, the colours only marginally spoiled by the Grand Pacific stained by the earth and rocks it inevitably picks up as it carves it way down the deep sided valley.

A superb moment in time was had by all. I know the experience hadn't been free, but it certainly felt like that after being robbed the day before on the train up the mountain, and I would have paid £200 just to be there. But as our Captain had said at the time, it was the best weather he had seen on the Bay for a long time....bottom line could have been that we saw nothing and left feeling cheated. That's life, I guess.

As we headed down the passage toward our last port of call, Ketchikan, the familiar sound of someone wailing 'Whale' led to numerous large bodies surging towards the nearest viewpoint, women and children last, drinks knocked down everywhere, beer mats flying, only for said whale to have disappeared under water, like they do, and I can safely say I still haven't seen one yet. Not that it bothers me much.

Ketchican modestly calls itself the 'Salmon Capital of the World' and keeps quiet about it probably being the wettest town in North America, affectionately referring to rain as being 'liquid sunshine'. Its population of some 8,000 can be effectively matched when the cruise ships hit town. This leads my thoughts to Dubrovnik, where at peak days there can be four cruise ships calling in, with at least 10,000 passengers entering the old walled town, which I guess is the size of your average garden centre. Perish the thought.

And guess what...it didn't rain and the sky was a magnificent City Blue as we wandered around the town and ended up on Creek Street, Alaska's most notorious red-light district from 1902 to 1950. The interesting zigzagging boardwalk on pilings above a creek supported over 30 'sporting houses', which have now been converted into shops selling what you would expect in a tourist destination, and no sign of my favourite shops, namely a bookshop or ironmongers. And how many jewellery shops does a place need, not to mention those that sell watches of every shape, size colour and creed?

Which leads me back to the subject of dogs, and my total abhorrence at owners who leave dog shit on our streets. As we watched salmon leap about on a river near the boardwalks my eye caught a sign which aptly read 'Dogs must be on leash when on boardwalk or person in control must remove fecal matter immediately'.

We had felt a bit cheated hearing about fellow holidaymakers seeing bears in the wild, and this was to be our last chance as we spent the equivalent cost of my first car, in buying a trip which they called an adventure, to visit nearby Herring Cove. No worries, if we didn't see one we would receive not our money back but a $80 credit. Super eh?

Certainly if I had read Trip Advisor before going I would have been a worried man, especially as this was not a 'prime' bear viewing area in the State, although bears were 'often' seen. And many customers were unhappy that no one had pointed out the five elevated swing bridges that led up to viewing platforms.

Worry not. This was an excellent, well organised trip and we saw lots of bears, big ones, mother and cubs and loads of salmon thrown in. Not literally, of course, and once for us, it was a case of 'right time, right place', as at this time of year (September) mature salmon, who had been spawned in the freshwater mountain streams before travelling down to sea, migrate back to the same rivers they were born. Only a few make it back, and for the bears it was easy picking. In many ways it was also sad to look down from our elevated position to see all the dead salmon, as those pesky bears prefer only to eat the brains and stomachs, and leave the rest.

On our last day at sea I resisted all the various activities on board to enjoy my favourite room, which was the library. To think I missed Mass, a 5k non-competitive walk around the ship's deck, and a seminar on 'Eat More to Weigh Less'. Additionally I could have learnt to Salsa, enjoy an Indonesian Tea Ceremony or learnt the art of towel folding with our room stewards. Naturally I didn't, however, miss Happy Hour in the Crows Nest, or what proved to be an excellent farewell dinner.

By the way, to prove how sad I sometimes can be, I spent most of the day reading an American book 'The $100 Start-Up' with a chapter on my unfinished mission of writing The One-Page Business Plan. In the author's words he says how the book will help you to learn how to achieve that perfect blend of passion and income to make work something you love. The originator, Chris Guillebeau, is described as a writer, entrepreneur and traveller. Good man, with attributes I strive for and maybe have marginally achieved, but entrepreneur 'No Way!'

Early doors we were back just as Vancouver woke up, and chauffeured (driver gratuity included) to our final destination for the next three days, a different Fairmont Hotel in Vancouver in which Queen Victoria and Prince Albert once stayed. Obviously if it had been good enough for them it was good enough for us, and when registering we heard those magic words, namely, "Mr Bullock you have been upgraded" although for the reason they didn't have a double room but would we settle for a twin bedded room? No problem, and in true North American 'bigness' our two singles were both as big as king-size beds, and in our Itinerary review of the hotel, our rooms had windows that open.

Bizarrely as it may seem, this posh hotel is not only dog friendly, it had a dog bed at reception which is shared by two K9 concierges, Mavis and Beau, both fine golden retrievers who you can take for a walk should you wish. Ok, if you don't believe me I suggest you visit t'internet.

In many ways it was strange to be back in Vancouver, in a different part of the city wondering what we were going to do over the next few days, and feeling slightly cheated that we were not at home celebrating the birth of our third grandson, Joshua, and only being able to see his handsome face on a mobile. So it was off to the HSBC Bank that I espied from our open window on the ninth floor, as I wanted to get rid of my American dollars. What a place, it had a pendulum in the banking hall the size of Big Ben, a cafe, and counterstaff.....unbelievable as it may seem...in abundance.

For the next couple of days we did the touristy things. We visited Gastown, named after Gassy Jack Deighton, a Yorkshire seaman who arrived there in the 1860's and opened the area's first saloon. Now an area being a mix of 'hip' contemporary fashion shops and interior design shops, with the usual cafes and restaurants, my lasting memory of the area (which is not a lot) is of the beggars on the streets, with cans of lager by their side. We passed by nearby Chinatown which looked a bit seedy. Granville Island, which in true form wasn't an island, was another place of call, and was another shopping experience being a public market, and a bit upmarket, if you get my flow, over the world famous Bury Market.

All shopped out, adventure called and my 30 minute float plane ride over Coal Harbour was cancelled in view of thunder and lightning, so to make up for my disappointment I called at a pub on my way back in Downtown, imaginatively and superbly named the Butcher & Bullock, and which boasted 28 types of beer. As one of these was not a Timothy Taylor Landlord I immediately walked out into what was a howling gale engulfing the city. And here's you thinking this was a non-fiction read.

We did get some thrills on FlyOver Canada, where in simulation mode you are sat in front of a giant screen, and for eight minutes, complete with wind, scent and mist you 'fly' over Canada from east to west over the spectacular scenery of this magnificent country. Even I felt a bit queasy as we dipped down after riding over the Rockies, whilst Elaine spent most of the time clutching the arm of the thoroughly decent gentleman to her left which wasn't me.

Our final trip saw us visit the popular Capilano Suspension Bridge, a wobbly crossing of some 140 metres which Elaine passed on, but she proudly hung on in there on the cliff walk, a high and narrow steel and glass walkway jutting out of the granite cliff some 70 feet above the river below, with not a bear or brainless salmon in sight.

If we have regrets following our time in the city one is emotional, the other fact. I expected it to be like Sydney which we loved and it wasn't, but I can only put that down to Vancouver not having the iconic buildings Sydney has, and certainly not the sunshine. But clearly we missed the opportunity to visit Vancouver Island, which everyone before, and since, has raved about. Put that down to choices and consequences.

So that was Vancouver. Unlike Manchester, the departure lounge did not disappoint, and with a fine glass of red in a proper size glass to hand, I was able to quietly reflect on the previous seventeen days, and what had been a superb holiday, with many highlights which I hope I have adequately shared with you. As hinted to previously, this was an area of the world where small equalled big, and big was just enormous and this applied to bodies, bellies, mouths, food, tips, taxes, cars, campervans, cameras I could go on. But most of all, and what was so pleasing, was that almost everyone we came into contact with as a tourist in a foreign land was BIG on service. It is, of course a cultural thing, and the inhabitants probably were just doing what came naturally, but it was so refreshing and undoubtedly helped to make a great holiday even greater.

PART THREE

LESLIE HENRY CHESTER DFC

1915 – 1989

L. H. Chester DFC

Prologue

ELAINE'S DAD WAS INDEED a funny chap, and not always in a humorous way. A journalist by trade, he married her Mum in Nottingham in July 1939, just two months before the outbreak of the Second World War. They met whilst ballroom dancing, and honeymooned in sunny Skegness. He was 24 at the time, son of a builder. He was the youngest of a family of four, his Mum dying shortly after he was born, and he was brought up by a close Aunt. He never spoke about his family, and in Elaine's memory they were hardly ever seen.

I always loved History at school, and my good grades in my 'A' levels secured my place at University, where I ended up majoring in fascism, which originated in Italy, and was favoured by Mussolini, who like my father-in-law, was once an Editor. Fascism was all about radical authoritarian nationalism, and the advent of the Great Depression of the 1930's provided an ideal background for Hitler, from 1933, to follow his dreams to rule the World. He got as far as Poland in 1939, and the rest, as they say, is history. Although we had been preparing for war, Germany was far more advanced in its military equipment and trained personnel, and but for the Battle of Britain, in the skies over the Channel between July and October 1940, who knows where we would have all ended up. Thanks go out to the RAF, and not forgetting also Hitler's decision to invade Russia, which certainly helped our cause.

Elaine also worked occasionally at her Dad's office, when he was Editor of the Melton Times. She noticed some headed notepaper, which read 'LH Chester DFC'. Upon enquiry she got rebuffed. When studying herself history at school, and indeed the Second World War, her class was encouraged to ask their parents about it to assist in their studies. Her reply from her father was "You don't want to know about that". All we ever got was the very occasional snippet.

And that takes us to 2003, when her Mum died, Les (and I never called him that you understand) having died from a heart attack in 1989. It was all in the bottom of the tatty old mahogany wardrobe they had got for a wedding present. There was his RAF hat, the DFC medal, many other medals, his Caterpillar Badge, and most significant of all for my purposes here, his RAF Flight Log Book.

I think it was John Lennon who once said "Life is what happens to you whilst you are busy making plans". Am sure he copied it from someone else, but it was always my intention to do some research on Les' flying career, and went as far as sharing this 'find' with a couple of former RAF personnel, one of whom had served in the war. To use his words: "For someone with a writer's flair, there's a book to be written about Squadron Leader Chester". And before I had the chance to meet with him, Alan Musgrove, he had died too. What follows is my humble attempt at this story.

First Tour of Duty

LES SIGNED UP IN May 1941, aged 25. Significantly, he volunteered. He was not conscripted. We have no idea as to his educational achievements, but he was undoubtedly intelligent and he mentioned to me once his time on Fleet Street. At the time he was probably a Sports Reporter with the Nottingham Evening Post. This would explain his love of Nottingham Forest, but not necessarily his love of boxing.

That May saw a lot of activity. The Luftwaffe spent seven days bombing over Liverpool, and later over Dublin, despite Ireland's neutrality. They also bombed the House of Commons. U-boats were active in the Atlantic where we experienced heavy losses, although on 27 May we sunk the German battleship, the famous Bismarck. Germany's largest battleship, it had a crew of almost 2,000.

Earlier in the month there was the bizarre episode when Rudolph Hess, Hitler's deputy, was captured in Scotland after bailing out of his plane. His aim was to broker peace with the UK.

I recall in 1979 reading a booked entitled 'The Murder of Rudolph Hess' in which the author Hugh Thomas argued quite convincingly that it was Hess' double that had been captured, and the 'real' Hess had been popped off because he opposed the German invasion of Russia, which commenced soon after. Subsequently I have been hooked on conspiracy theories, and Hugh Thomas was a Professor of History when I was at Reading University, and a hero of mine at the time. We had many a long conversation, and he certainly was a great, but highly intelligent, eccentric.

The strategic air campaign was, in essence, made up as it went along. Volunteers like Les were signing up to join the RAF and had no idea where they would end up. Many of them would have dreamed of becoming a fighter pilot, but by the Spring of 1941 Fighter Command's hour had passed and the air war now belonged to Bomber Command, and especially the four engine heavies being the Stirlings, Halifaxes and especially the Lancasters (often referred to as the 'Lancs'). A well-oiled training system soon evolved and produced a continuous stream of competent and well prepared airmen. And boy were they needed.

There were basically six jobs for which volunteers could be considered namely pilot, navigator, engineer, bomb-aimer, wire-less operator and air gunners, of which there were two. After initial vetting he would have been sent to an Aircrew Selection Centre. Initially he would have faced a series of academic tests, which were marked on the spot, and if you failed you were sent home. Next day was a rigorous medical and finally an interview in front of a panel of three senior officers. Successful candidates were sworn in, given their RAF number, and then, anticlimactically sent home to wait to be summoned. This period of deferred service could last many months, and a chap called Ken Newman, who joined up at the same time as Les, didn't see any action until the spring of 1944, some three years later.

Les didn't have to wait long at all, and his first operational flight was in a Lancaster as Wireless Operator over Bremen on 25 June 1942, even so, some 12 months after volunteering.

His training will have been a mixture of theory and practice, starting at Air Crew Reception Centres, and more latterly in Operational Training Units. In Les' case these were in Penrhos, Wales and RAF Kinloss, in the north of Scotland and, throughout the War, the primary OTU unit in the country. The theoretical training in airmanship, meteorology, mathematics, Morse code and aircraft recognition was tough, and an 80% success rate was needed to pass. Les got 84%, and his log book records this as being only 'Average'.

How he ended up being a Wireless Operator on Lancs I have no idea. He will have been selected into this trade as a result of his aptitude in training, and may have had something to do with his life as a journalist. It certainly seems to me to have been preferable to the role of the gunners who seem to have had the worst job of all. They lived in metal and Perspex turrets, washed by whistling winds that could freeze them to their guns. Additionally they had the huge task of defending their mates, constantly scanning the night for flak and enemy. Wireless Operators trained also as gunners, and the log book reveals that Les received an exam mark of 78%, his trainer remarking this as being, yes you've guessed, 'Average'. In fact, his only success seems to have been in Night Vision, in which he scored 'Above Average'. Notwithstanding, learning these two 'skills' meant training was longer than any other aircrew trade, attending also a 'wireless school', and the dropout rate was usually high.

The wireless operator, who unlike the rear gunners used to roast because he was so close to the inner engine, according to Bruce Lewis, who was one, and who reveals in his book that he was also the practical man of the crew, always ready in an emergency with a screwdriver and bits of wire. My memory of Les was that he was exactly that, being a bit of a 'Bodge-It' man, often seen filling rotting window frames with filler, and thereby only delaying the inevitable. Bruce reveals that it was a lonely existence, mentally isolated from other members of the crew for long periods whilst he strained to listen through the static in his headphones for faint but vital signals. These told him the aircraft's position which he passed on to the Navigator. He also manned the radar monitor which warned of the approach of enemy night-fighters. This again may explain the character I came to know, but never knew if you get my drift.

Prior to his first mission, Les flew a total of 176 hours, 68 hours of which at night. Whilst I will be sharing a few more statistics with you, incredibly by the end of the war 8,090 Bomber Command personnel died in training accidents, and 4,203 were injured. Questions were asked, but never answered, I believe.

As Basil Fawlty famously said in that sketch to his German guests "But you started it!"; this war was the first seen whereby aeroplanes were used in large numbers against large population areas to smash an enemy's capacity to make war by destroying its industry and demoralising its civilians. The German Blitz of 1940-41 of this country saw 41,000 civilians killed, and some 137,000 injured. Our response, up to 1942, however had not been effective. We had small planes, small bombs and especially primitive navigation aids. Losses were high, and some 2,300 aircraft had been lost with very little to show for it. It was almost impossible to know whether a raid had been successful or not, with a lot of bombs just landing on countryside. The ports of Hamburg, Kiel and Bremen suffered only nominal damage, with the Ruhr largely untouched. The low point came on 7 November 1941 when a record 169 flew to bomb Berlin, only half got anywhere near it, and we lost 21 planes that night. Whilst the war propaganda machine was saying one thing, Churchill was becoming increasingly concerned. Enter Leslie Chester.

I jest, of course. I am talking about Arthur Harris, who in

February 1942 took over Bomber Command. The press christened him 'Bomber Harris' whilst in the RAF he was affectionately known as 'Butch', an abbreviation from Butcher. Right time, right man, the period after the Berlin disaster had seen a pause in major operations to give the force a breathing space. The Americans had joined the war following the attack on Pearl Harbour in the December, and the Germans were preoccupied with fighting Russia, who then later become an ally. The first of the new four engine heavies, including the Lancs, came into service, as did the new navigation system called the Gee, being soon followed by the Oboe. However, these improvements whilst assisting in getting the aircraft to the target area, did not pinpoint the target to be hit.

Butch's first change in operations was to end the practice of splitting up the force and sending it to bomb two or three targets over a protracted period. The principle now was to despatch as many aircraft that could be mustered against one target, aiming for saturation. He also argued for bombs to be followed by four pound incendiaries to float down on shattered buildings to start fires that would feed on the winds whipped up by the blasts.

Les was stationed at RAF Conningsby, Lincolnshire, which is reported to have been one of the better appointed bases in the country. He would have loved the 'new' Avro Lancaster, in which he flew for almost all of his time on operational service, which was seen at the time to be a masterpiece of military aviation design. An incredible 7,377 were built between 1941 and early 1946, of which over half were either lost, destroyed or written off in crashes. And they were built in Oldham! Moreover, I can only guess he would be pleased at last to join in the action, and in joining 106 Squadron, which had just appointed to command, Wing Commander Guy Gibson. A strict disciplinarian, he is well known for leading the famous Dam Buster Raid of May 16/17 1943, and who signed

Les' Log Book on eight occasions.

If you are looking for a hero, I recommend you look no further than Guy Gibson. He had completed over 120 missions before taking over 106 Squadron at the incredibly tender age of 23, with whom he completed another 46 sorties, including the Dam Buster Raid for which he received the Victoria Cross. After that he was 'pensioned off' and gave talks in America. He longed, however, to return to action, and flew Mosquitos over Germany, where in 1944, his plane allegedly crashed through lack of fuel. I say 'allegedly' as there remains a theory that he was shot down by friendly fire, by, of all things, a Lancaster Bomber. He was aged 26.

Again, and we did not share it, I wonder often what Les would have thought when we named our first son Guy. The story goes that whilst Elaine was a teacher at Bolton School there was a boy in her class called Guy Mathieson and she liked the name. And his brother was also at the School. He was called Ross.

I also wonder what would have been going through Les' head in the afternoon of 25 June 1942, during the briefing that would have preceded his first operational flight that evening. The war had entered a new era three weeks earlier with the first 'thousand' raid on Cologne, Germany's third largest City. In fact all together 1047 aircraft took part, dropping 1455 bombs. Devastation was immense and indiscriminate.

On 25 June, Les, on his first operational flight, was the second wireless operator, presumably 'learning on the job'. He took part in the third and last thousand raid targeting Bremen, comprising every available aircraft in Bomber Command which totalled 1067, of which 96 were Lancs. Assisted by the Gee navigation system, Les was in the group that destroyed a Folke-Wulf aircraft factory. Overall the whole operation was deemed to have been 'useful', with 28 aircraft not returning. Les, in his last flight as a second wireless operator, took part in a smaller raid on Bremen on 29 June.

On his first mission as a fully-fledged Wireless Operator, on 31 July, disaster nearly struck. The mission was over Dusseldorf in Western Germany, an industrial centre for chemicals, steel and machinery. On the outward journey over the Dutch coast, considerable trouble developed in the Lanc's fuel system. Despite this they dropped 11 bombs on its target in the face of heavy anti-aircraft fire and they were hit by flak. On the way back both starboard engines failed, but they flew on and some 50 miles from base both port engines failed. At 3,000 ft Les and four other crew members were ordered to bail out, whilst the pilot and second pilot remained on the aircraft in an attempt to save it. They were able to get fuel to the port engines to restart them, and despite atrocious conditions they landed safely at another base, without any damage to the aircraft. The pilot, Sergeant Lace, received the Distinguished Flying Medal (DFM) for his efforts. He survived the war, and in peace time got a job as a pilot with British Airways at Heathrow.

By surviving in this way Les became eligible for membership of the International Caterpillar Club, all of whose members have had their lives saved through use of parachute. We have his gilt gold badge in the form of a caterpillar and no longer an inch in length. The official membership of this worldwide organisation, established in 1920, is in excess of 100,000, and does not include the Luftwaffe airmen who carried the same Leslie Irwin designed parachute that saved my father-in-law's life.

Spare a thought also for Flight Sergeant Nicolas Alkemade, who was a Rear Gunner in a Lancaster attacked over Berlin in 1944. With his leg shattered, and his parachute burnt, he had two choices. He could stay in the plane as it dropped to earth or he could jump. He chose the latter and began the three and a half miles to earth. Incredibly when he opened his eyes, he was not in heaven but in Westphalia. Through great fortune he had fallen through some pine trees and into a snow drift, both of which had cushioned the impact. As he didn't use a parachute he wasn't eligible to join the Caterpillar Club. Rules are Rules, you know.

The bigger the planes, the bigger the bombs they could carry, and in theory the more damage they could do in meeting the objectives of this period of mass bombing. The RAF had started the war with poor quality bombs that were more metal than charge, and often failed to go off. In the spring of 1941 they began to be replaced by a new series of high capacity blast bombs, led by the 4,000-pound bomb, known as a 'cookie'. A green-painted cylinder, the size of a dustbin, they had seemed to have no aerodynamics at all, but their thin casings enabled them to contain three quarters of their weight in explosives.

Les' next three operations in August saw him in Lancs dropping those cookies over Germany, whilst on 28 August in a night flight over Nuremburg, something extraordinary happened, and which led to the longest report in his Log Book which I repeat exactly as it was written (the brackets are mine):

> *"8,000lb H.E (High Explosive) jettisoned from 15,000 ft after attack by E/A (enemy aircraft) near Darmstadt. Rear and M/U (mid-upper) turrets U/S (unserviceable) R.G. (presumably fellow crew member) wounded. M.U. Gunner burnt extinguishing fires. Landed on burst tyres."*

Then as an aside he reports *"First crew to take an 8,000 bomb over Germany and return"*.

The bombs were getting bigger, and the 8,000lb was basically two 4,000lbs attached together. The research I have undertaken through Wikipedia reveals the development of the bombs and reports that the first 8,000lb bomb was dropped by 15 Squadron Lancaster over Berlin on 2 December 1943, some

15 months later. Now who do you believe? Les was a man of detail and correctness, and his record of events was confirmed by no other than Guy Gibson. No case to argue where I am coming from. Nevertheless, whilst no doubt Les was delighted to survive this operation, as was usual the Pilot would have ordered they get rid of all their bombs indiscriminately in the event they crash landed. Where this highly destructive bomb landed we will never know.

Notably also, a sortie the day before over Kassel saw Les' plane attacked by a JU88 of the Luftwaffe, which they shot down. Also this month a new formation of huge significance came into being, namely the Path Finder Force, more of which later.

By this time Les had undertaken nine sorties. The chance of surviving a whole tour of operations, thirty missions, was just 1 in 4, worse than any other branch of the armed services. A further 10,000 escaped from doomed aircraft, many of whom ended up in Prisoner of War Camps. And he had just started.

Les was to fly in another 24 missions in his first tour of duty which ended in January 1943, being over France, Germany and Northern Italy, during which his plane was hit by flak on six occasions. Often suffering from hydraulic failure, they invariably landed in different bases from where they had taken off. On one notable occasion in October, following dropping a 4,000lb bomb over Aachen, their Lancaster's starboard engine failed at 7,000 ft, some 40 miles from base. They crash landed near Nottingham, the aircraft being destroyed by fire and explosion. The pilot, Sgt Lace, was awarded bar to his DFM.

The majority of Les' flying time was at night. However, he took part on 17 October in a famous daylight raid against a factory in Le Creusot, in France. There was produced heavy guns, railway engines and tanks. He was in one of the 94 Lancasters taking part, of which 93 returned safely. For 300 miles of the journey the Lancasters flew at tree level over the French countryside, no German fighters attacked them, and the greatest danger was from birds; 4 aircraft were damaged and 2 men injured in bird strikes. Nearly 140 tons of bombs were dropped. In the same raid, there was also an attack on a transformer Station, including one Guy Gibson, who bombed and machine gunned it from 500ft, this being mentioned in his citation for a Distinguished Service Order a month later. Les returned to base, after his longest flight of almost 11 hours. He was back in the air the next day.

Les' last mission saw him bombing over Essen, the third time he had been there in eight days. That was 11 January 1943, having completed 33 trips (in his parlance in his Log Book) with flying time 201 hours and 15 minutes. There would have been no ceremony, and in true military fashion his crew would have probably been told by their Wing Commander "Hey you lads – you're finished!" That was it for six months.

In a Supplement to the London Gazette in August 1943, Leslie Henry Chester (148035) is recorded as receiving the Distinguished Flying Cross (DFC). It arrived at his home in Nottingham in a little brown box, with a copied note from King George and worded "I greatly regret that I am unable to give you personally the award which you have so well earned. I now send it to you with my congratulations and my best wishes for your future happiness."

Ground Time

L ES WOULD HAVE GONE HOME to Nottingham to be reunited with his wife, and then posted to a non-operational unit as a trainer of new recruits. Never one to suffer fools gladly I can only guess he would be a no-nonsense type of instructor, but if he was like others in the same situation he would have missed the action. It is of surprise that, being a journalist, he never wrote of his experiences, as many have, and as such, whilst I have written as best I can about the missions he undertook, what was it really like?

Based at RAF Conningsby would be about 2,500 personnel. Accommodation would have been primitive in their billets, with only the Officers having their own quarters. Food was basic, and when not flying they lived on Spam, dried eggs, sausages and lumps of nameless fish. Apparently there were cartons of raisins everywhere to help yourself, vitamin pills and cigarettes were freely available. There was the mess, where there were papers to read and tea to drink. There was also a cinema.

An average day would see him get up, and probably go down to his aircraft to do what Wireless Operators did, change the accumulators and generally make sure everything was set up properly. The crew wouldn't know from one day to the next whether they were flying or not that night, or where they would be going. It was left for the Signal Officer to say "You're working tonight!" One crew member, Bill Wareham, a W/O in 467 Squadron wrote when he heard this said, of the intense fear, which you didn't show. It was hidden in different ways; some would crack jokes, others tended to be very quiet. Les once shared with Elaine that he could often tell which crews wouldn't be coming back.

Briefing generally began at 3pm, starting with the navigators and pilots, then the bomb aimers and lastly the wireless operators who would be given the frequencies for that night, these being on rice paper.

The crew still didn't know where they were going until the whole squadron was briefed later, and the curtain was pulled back behind which would be an enormous map. They would have guessed if they were in for a long haul by how much fuel had been put in their aircraft. The briefing would start with the Group Captain, followed by the Group Wing Commander who would explain how many 'waves' there would be, and what was their target and tactics for the night. It would end with the weather 'bloke' who advised of the conditions for the night, and apparently he was invariably wrong.

Les, extreme left, with fellow crew members

When the rockets went up it was time to get in their aircraft, and start up. Wareham talks about the feeling in his stomach, the whole thing just churning over. Another former rear gunner revealed that 'they were scared witless'. The crew always boarded in the same order. The noise of the four engines starting up was immense, and they were invariably waved off by ground crew and staff. The aim was to get to 20,000 feet as soon as possible, and by the time they got to the Dutch coast the action would start, and enemy aircraft would be threatening.

The object was always to 'get in and get out'. Once they had reached the target it was the bomb aimers job to get rid of the bombs as quickly as possible and turn home. Invariably they were at their most vulnerable then, as the plane would slow to what seemed a crawl, with flak everywhere. They would hang there for what seemed an eternity, the crew desperate to hear 'Bombs gone!' With the load dropped and half their fuel used the aircraft could travel a lot faster, and with enemy fighters, the Junker 88, about, it was time for the air-gunners to come into action, as the plane swung round and headed home.

Back at base, say five hours later, and safely landed, Wareham talks of it being incredibly difficult to describe the feeling of touching down. And all of us have flown back from our holidays and will know that feeling well, and we have just sat there, eating and drinking and being entertained! The crew would have been picked up and taken for a briefing, before which they would have received a cup of tea (they were British after all) laced with rum. They would be asked all the detail of the mission, with the Wireless Operator being quizzed about whether he had received all the Bomber Command messages, the wind speeds etc. Then they would get rid of their gear, go back to the mess, have some bacon and eggs, and then to bed. At least they knew they wouldn't be flying the next day as they would have work to do on their aircraft. But the day after that......

Occasionally the men could let their hair down, and the messes were the social hub, in which off-duty airmen could go for a quiet drink or a full-scale piss-up if the mood took them. Despite being a strong disciplinarian Guy Gibson recognised that his young men lived in a time of incredible strain, and the licensed boisterousness that often followed he thought built the team spirit which sustained the whole business of bombing. Surprisingly the RAF took a relaxed view on alcohol consumption to the extent that Bomber Harris felt the need to justify the frequent mention of 'parties' and 'drunks' in Guy Gibson's diaries. It is told that war time restrictions meant the beer available to them was notoriously flat and watery, but not the whisky. In all my time I never saw Les with a pint in his hand, but he enjoyed the occasional whisky, albeit with a dash of water!

Les had two months off, before joining OTU Cottesmore as an Instructor in March 1943. Who knows what would have been going through his head as he would have spent quality time with his wife at home but no doubt kept in touch, as best they could in those days, with his fellow crew members. He instructed the new intake in Wellington Bombers.

1943 had started well for Bomber Harris, receiving the green light at a conference of the Allies' leaders in Casablanca in a directive 'to pursue the progressive destruction of the German military, industrial and economic system, and the undermining of the morale of the German people to a point where their capacity for armed resistance is fatally weakened'. With more trained crew, and nearly 1200 aircraft, this year saw the Battle of the Ruhr, the Dambusters raid and extensive bombing over Hamburg and Berlin. Known as the 'Big City' between 18 November 1943 and March 24 1944, a total of 16 raids devastated over 2000 acres of Berlin, killing 6000 inhabitants and rendering one and a half million Germans homeless. The cost to the Allies was 492 lost planes, and crews 'missing'

CHAPTER 3

Second Tour of Duty

THE LAST RAID ON BERLIN had seen the return to action of Leslie Chester DFC, who was now on a second tour of duty and had joined 156 Squadron which was based at RAF Upwood in Cambridgeshire. He left behind his wife Kathleen.

156 Squadron was in fact one of four squadrons that made up the famous Path Finder Force. Its purpose was quite succinct – to spearhead main bombing sorties and locate and mark the target accurately before the main bomber stream arrived. Everyone who flew with the Pathfinders volunteered to do so, and those who joined were the very best at their trade, whatever crew position they occupied. It was indeed to become a crack force.

It was certainly literally a baptism of fire for Les' return on 24 March over Berlin. That night, of the 811 aircraft involved, 72 were lost. Known as the 'night of the strong winds', which had not been predicted, the aircraft became scattered and were blown into several well defended locations. 50 of the 72 aircraft lost were destroyed by flak. With these, and other considerable losses for the Allies, the Battle of Berlin had not brought Germany to its knees as Bomber Harris has predicted. Questions were again being asked as to the effectiveness of

Bomber Command.

Thanks to a superb web-site I am able to follow every mission Les undertook for the rest of the year, the target areas, the successes and, unfortunately, the losses incurred. 6 June 1944 saw the greatest invasion force of all time in D-Day, which saw Bomber Command support, before by August, with the allied armies flooding across Europe towards Germany, concentration was again seen against Germany's oil refineries and remaining war industries.

On 26 August Les took part in a massive attack over the industrial town of Russelsheim, whose Opel factory made aeroplane parts. According to the website the Pathfinders did their job in ten minutes, and the convoy dropped 2000 pound bombs reducing the factory to rubble, destroying the historic city and half its housing. Les' plane was hit by 'friendly' fire from another Lancaster, but returned home safely. 15 other Lancasters weren't so lucky and were destroyed. What followed is known as the Russelsheim Massacre, and which is so terrible as to defy description and which I will not share with you.

Les' last mission on 17 December was over Ulm, and was also the last RAF raid on the city, with its two large factories, some important industries and military barracks. A total of 1449 bombs were dropped during the 25-minute raid, and which saw 2 of the 317 Lancs not return. Les did return, of course, and would have been home for Christmas.

In his second tour of duty Acting Flight Lieutenant Leslie Chester had flown in 28 missions and 206 hours and 35 minutes of flying time. He was soon to be awarded bar to DFC. His active days were effectively over, but he remained in the RAF for the rest of the war, and qualified as a Signals Leader in June 1945.

Bomber Command flew missions against the Germans almost every day and night between September 1939 to May

1945; an incredible feat of courage and endurance. The chance of surviving a tour of duty, usually 30 missions, was just 1 in 4. Les completed two tours, of course. Maybe he was good at his job, in a good team or just lucky. Probably all three, but he survived. 55,573 didn't, that being nearly half the strength of Bomber Command. Put into context that was a lower survival chance than of a British infantry officer on the Western Front in the First World War.

The story doesn't end here, as you are probably aware. The policy of area bombing inevitably led to the devastation of its victims, many of them inevitably civilians, and has led to the vilification of Bomber Command. Whilst strategic bombing was aimed at munitions and aircraft factories, oil plants and transport links, it was also intended to break the spirit of the German people. Over 500,000 died in air raids.

Throughout the conflict there were those who opposed the bombing as an immoral way of waging war. It is to Churchill's eternal shame that, having ignored these protests and supported Bomber Harris to the hilt, he then backtracked. In his victory address to the nation, he conspicuously made no mention whatsoever of Bomber Command's contribution. Thereafter, creeping guilt rather than pride became our default position about the war, and some Germans even accused us of being war criminals. Bomber Harris even became a hate figure for the Left, and when a statue was erected to him in 1992, pacifists smeared it with red paint.

Meanwhile the men themselves kept their heads down, baffled and hurt. To a degree this may be why Les never talked about his war days, other than the odd throw away remark. It may, however, have been his way of coping with what he had seen and gone through. Chapter closed. There was no such thing as post-traumatic stress syndrome counselling then.

I was pleased, therefore, in her Jubilee Year 2012, the Queen unveiled the official memorial to the men of Bomber

Command in London's Green Park. Good on her. An old debt will have at least been acknowledged. It can never be repaid.

Epilogue

LES RETURNED TO CIVILIAN LIFE and to the Nottingham Post, where he gained promotion from Sports Reporter to Deputy Editor. He subsequently in the late 1960's applied for and succeeded in becoming Managing Editor & Secretary of the Melton Mowbray Times, being elected to the Board in 1971. He retired in 1976 and spent his time reading, gardening (under sufferance) and enjoying his great love of caravanning. He was 74, when he died of a heart attack.

We will never know how his five years in the RAF, as a young man in his twenties, determined the character I knew, and Elaine knew as his daughter. An intensely private individual, you certainly would not mess with him. He rarely showed any emotion, but deep down we believed he cared.

He was a disciplinarian with an eye for detail, as befitted his profession. There was little hope for any Reporter who presented him with copy containing grammatical errors.

One of Elaine's lasting memories of her father was she was working in his office one day. Her Dad took a call from a young Reporter who rang in and said he had injured himself at the weekend playing football and wouldn't be in for work that week. Having ascertained that he could walk, Les said that if he wasn't in the Office that morning he would be sacked. Naturally he appeared later, and having just read what Les had gone through during the War, you can understand why he said what he did.

As a further postscript, my own father was in the RAF during the war, although at sea. He worked on the Motor Torpedo Boats who rushed to the rescue of airmen who had parachuted into the sea. And as you would expect...he never talked about it.